P9-DMD-382

WITHDRAWN

make your own **ZOO**

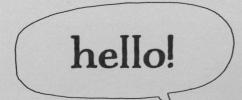

hello!

make your own **zoo**

35 projects for kids using everyday cardboard packaging

Tracey Radford

CICO BOOKS
LONDON NEW YORK

LONDON PUBLIC LIBRARY

For Sam, Kit, and Daisy,
my inspirational Zookeepers

Published in 2015 by CICO Books
An imprint of Ryland Peters & Small Ltd
20–21 Jockey's Fields   341 E 116th St
London WC1R 4BW   New York, NY 10029

www.rylandpeters.com

10 9 8 7 6 5 4 3 2 1

Text © Tracey Radford 2015
Design and photography © CICO Books 2015

The author's moral rights have been asserted. All rights
reserved. No part of this publication may be reproduced,
stored in a retrieval system, or transmitted in any form
or by any means, electronic, mechanical, photocopying,
or otherwise, without the prior permission of
the publisher.

A CIP catalog record for this book is available from
the Library of Congress and the British Library.

ISBN: 978 1 78249 256 6

Printed in China

Editor: Jane Birch
Designer: Louise Leffler
Photographers: Martin Norris and Terry Benson
Template illustrations: Stephen Dew

In-house editor: Anna Galkina
In-house designer: Fahema Khanam
Art director: Sally Powell
Head of production: Patricia Harrington
Publishing manager: Penny Craig
Publisher: Cindy Richards

Contents

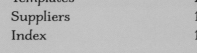

Introduction

It all started with a lion I made with my daughter Daisy. You see, the lion was lonely, so we made a lioness to keep him company... followed by a giraffe and a zebra. Then, of course, they needed somewhere to live... and that really is how the Zoo came about. It was an idea that grew and grew. For me, the most fun crafts to do with kids are often the ones that keep on growing; the ones that aren't just about making, but about creating little worlds—whether those worlds are full of safari animals or a whole bunch of penguins! I'm also a big believer in using things everyone has lying about at home. The Zoo animals are made from ordinary cardboard packaging that usually ends up in your recycling container. It's cheap, environmentally friendly, and it's all just sitting there, waiting for you to transform it into something...

Crafting with egg cartons and cardboard tubes is not an exact science though—sizes, shapes, and colors vary—so please don't worry if your animal looks different from the picture, that's perfectly okay. It's about working with what you've got, and adapting if you need to. No two animals will look the same—they'll all have their own personalities. Remember, it's *your* Zoo. You will notice that a lot of techniques are repeated in different projects. Some, like slot cutting, are more tricky than others, but once confident cutters have got the hang of this, there'll be no stopping them! If you feel your child isn't quite ready for slot cutting, you can always glue or paint on eyes, ears, and beaks instead. These options are explained in the step-by-step instructions for the relevant projects.

Daisy and I have had a real adventure making the Zoo—we hope you do too!

SAFETY MATTERS

The projects in this book are for you and your child to do together and are suitable for children approximately six years and older. Always keep a close eye on children while you are helping them and never leave children alone with scissors or glue, even for a few minutes.

Tools & materials

Hopefully you'll find most of what you need around the house—but, before you get going, here's a list of a few essentials, plus some handy tips and techniques to check through first.

Scissors

Kids will get plenty of scissor practice! Cutting is a key part of most of the projects. Sometimes it'll be challenging, like learning to pierce holes, cut slots, or snip out small shapes. This book is for children aged six and over but, even then, scissor skills vary. You are the best judge of how much help to give your child. Always supervise any cutting.

As well as a good pair of scissors—called general-purpose scissors in the projects—you'll need some small, sharp ones; this is really important. Straight-edged nail scissors are ideal, because their short blades make it much easier to control cutting out small shapes, and they're sharp enough to make holes for slots. When a project specifies small scissors, these are the ones you'll need. Embroidery or needlework scissors are good too. When a particular type of scissors is not specified, use whichever size you feel most comfortable with.

The best technique I've found to help children use these small scissors safely to make holes is to keep the scissors closed and press down firmly on the cardboard, twisting slightly from side to side until the tip pierces through. You might find putting a ball of modeling clay (plasticine) behind the cardboard helps, as it gives something to push against. This can be especially useful for piercing small slots for ears and eyes. Bear in mind, the more cutting you let children do, the better their scissor skills will be!

Glue

The best glue to use is craft (PVA) glue, which is widely available. It's washable and easy to paint over. The problem sometimes is it can be quite runny, so glued-on pieces may slip. A top tip to get around this is to pour a small amount of glue—about ¼ in. (5 mm)—into an old, clean yogurt container or a jar. Leave, uncovered, somewhere out of reach. After about a day, it should start thickening up—this will happen more quickly in warm conditions. The longer you leave it, the tackier it gets. In the instructions, this is what tacky glue refers to. Keep an eye on it, and either top up as you use it, or have a few containers on the go at once.

Watered-down craft (PVA) glue is great for brushing over small newspaper pieces to cover holes or cracks, in a similar way to making papier-mâché. A glue stick is very handy for sticking down paper, so it doesn't get too wet and crinkly—for example, grass for scenery (see page 110), or Mr. Crocodile's teeth (see page 50). When it comes to gluing pipe cleaners, a stronger, all-purpose adhesive works best.

Paint

Ready-mixed kids' poster or acrylic paints are what you need. Tempera-based paints are good too. All the colors you need to paint the animals can be made from red, yellow, blue, white, and black. Usually a pack of six paints will include a nice bright green as well.

Paint brushes

A decent selection of different-sized brushes helps. Small brushes are good for things like painting birds (see chapter 4) and for adding details such as stripes and spots, and bigger brushes are ideal for speeding up scenery painting.

Pens

A good black felt-tip pen or marker with a medium tip is great for drawing faces. A black gel pen or fine black felt-tip pen works best for the smaller creatures; these are interchangeable, so you can choose which one you prefer.

Cardboard tubes

Toilet-paper tubes are especially useful, but gather up a few paper-towel tubes and giftwrap tubes too. Make sure you have a good mix of different tube widths.

Egg cartons

Again, not all egg cartons are exactly alike. Some are better for cutting out a good egg-cup shape (the molded piece that holds the egg) and others might be better for cones (the pointy cardboard pieces in the middle of a carton that protect the eggs). You'll find some egg-cup pieces are squarer on the bottom, or have shorter sides, while some cones are larger or less pointy than others, and some cartons don't have the cones at all.

Please don't worry if your cartons look different—this is the nature of this kind of craft; half the fun is making the most of what you've got and tweaking here and there if you need to. It's not just the egg cups and cones that are useful—every part of the carton gets used in this book! If it's not so easy to find cardboard egg cartons in your neighborhood stores, you can order them online. I know this is an added expense, but with careful cutting, you should be able to get a couple of animal heads, a few monkeys, and some flying parrots from one carton!

> ## RECYCLING
> Nearly every zoo animal is made from either cardboard tubes, egg cartons, or cereal boxes—or all three. It pays to have a good collection of recyclables because they vary in size and shape.

Cereal-box cardboard

Another kids' craft staple. The only drawback is the shiny side is often difficult to paint. If you do want both sides painted, then rub the shiny side with sandpaper to remove the sheen. This makes it easier for the paint to grip to the surface. You may need to apply a few coats of paint. Alternatively, use a glue stick to glue a plain piece of paper to the shiny side, and weigh this down under something heavy, like a pile of books, while it dries. You'll notice I often use cardboard from an egg carton lid instead of cereal-box cardboard, especially for the smaller creatures. This is because it's usually easier to paint both sides. Pull off any labels, and paint the top and underside of the lid before cutting, so the wet paint doesn't touch or stick to surfaces while it dries.

chapter 1
safari

Lions, tigers, hippos,
there are animals galore!
So much for you to make and do,
come see what fun's in store...

Brian the Lion

Roll up to the zoo! Roll up to the zoo!
And hear the lion roar!
Though, as he's fond of sleeping,
it'll probably be a snore...

You will need

Toilet-paper tube

Approx. 8 x 8 in. (20 x 20 cm)
cereal-box cardboard, cut in half

Paw template (see page 124)

General-purpose scissors

Tacky glue (see page 8)

Yellow and brown paint

Paint brush

Ruler

Pencil

2 paperclips

Circular shapes, such as a
drinking glass and a spice jar, to
use as templates

Black felt-tip pen

1 Measure 3 in. (8 cm) from the top of the toilet-paper tube and mark the point with a pencil, then draw a line all the way around.

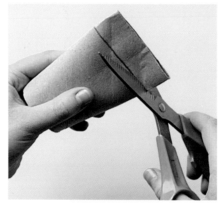

2 Press the sides of the marked end of the tube together and use scissors to cut along the line.

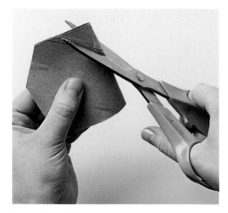

3 Still pressing the sides of the tube together, snip off the corners.

4 Glue the two sides of the tube together well using tacky glue, then use the paperclips to hold the sides together while the glue dries. This will be the body of the lion.

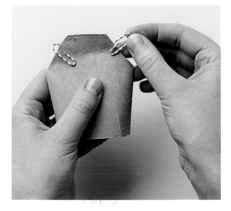

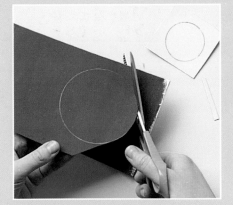

5 When the glue is dry, remove the paperclips. Paint the body and one of the pieces of the cereal-box cardboard yellow. Paint the other half of cardboard brown.

6 When the paint is dry, use a drinking glass as a template for the lion's mane. Place the glass on the brown cardboard, and draw around it with a pencil. On the yellow cardboard, draw around something smaller, like a spice jar, to make the face. Then use the paw template to draw two paws, also on the yellow cardboard.

7 Cut out the circles and paws and cut a thin strip of yellow cardboard to make the tail.

roar!

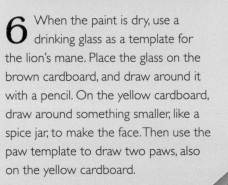

TIP
Keep any leftover yellow-painted cardboard as it can be used to make the tiger on page 18 and the lioness on page 15.

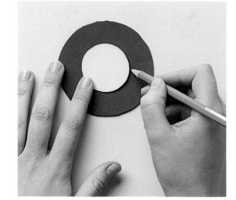

8 Position the lion's face on the mane and draw around it with a pencil. Set the face to one side while you make the mane.

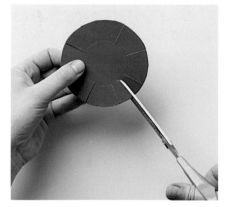

9 To make the mane, cut up to the pencil line only. Start by making cuts at the half-way points of the circle. Then cut half-way between these cuts, and then half-way between those cuts, and so on. This will keep the mane even and help avoid accidentally chopping bits of cardboard off... though a few gaps won't matter!

10 Use a black felt-tip pen to draw a face on the yellow circle and claws on the paws.

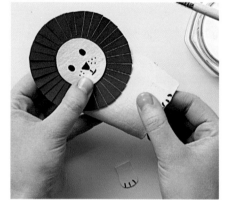

11 Using tacky glue, stick the face on to the mane and then glue the mane to the lion's body. Glue the paws to the front of the body.

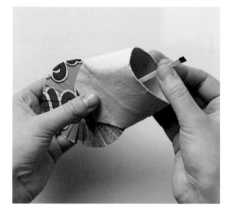

12 Color one end of the tail with the felt-tip pen. Glue the other end inside the tube. When the glue is dry, bend the tail into position.

Lottie the Lioness

The lion thinks that he's in charge,
but everybody knows
It's the lioness who calls the shots
and keeps him on his toes!

You will need

1 toilet-paper tube (approx. 4 in./10 cm long), a narrow one, if possible

Approx. 4 × 8 in. (10 × 20 cm) cereal-box cardboard

Hind leg and head templates (see page 124)

General-purpose scissors

Tacky glue (see page 8)

Yellow paint

Paint brush

Ruler

Pencil

Ball of modeling clay

Black felt-tip pen

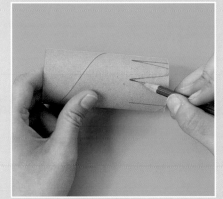

1 At one end of the toilet-paper tube, measure two points 1½ in. (4 cm) apart. Mark these with a pencil and from these points draw two lines each 1 in. (3 cm) long.

2 With the pencil, mark a point half-way between these two lines at the top. Draw down from the top of one of the lines to the edge of the tube, curving around, for a front paw, and then up to the mid-point. Repeat for the other leg.

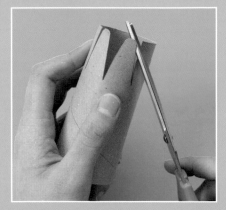

3 Cut along the lines and around the paws.

4 Place the paw side of the tube on a flat surface and, using the palm of your hand, push down gently on the top of the tube—just enough to flatten the bottom a little and stop it rocking.

5 Straight above the paws, mark two lines 1 in. (3 cm) long and 1 in. (3 cm) apart on the top surface of the tube. Cut along the lines with scissors.

6 To make up the body, fold the two side flaps in and snip off any bits getting in the way.

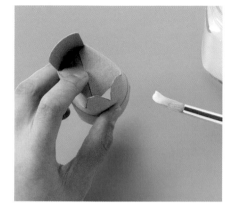

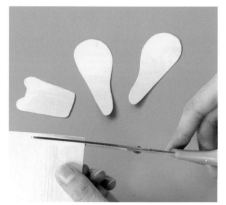

7 Using tacky glue, stick the two side flaps together and weigh them down with a ball of modeling clay, or something similar. Don't glue the top flap down.

8 When the glue is dry, paint the body and the cereal-box cardboard yellow.

9 Place the hind leg and head templates on the cardboard and draw around them with a pencil. Be sure to draw both a left leg and a right leg. Cut them out and cut out a small strip of cardboard for a tail.

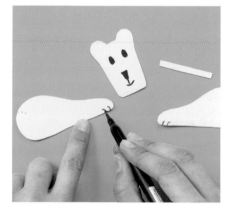

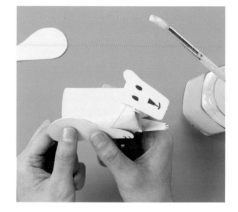

10 Using a black felt-tip pen, color the end of the tail in, draw claws on the front paws, and draw a face on the head.

11 Bend the top flap down and stick on the head, cutting away any corners that peep out.

12 Glue the left and right hind legs onto the body; this will stop the body rolling about. Glue the end of the tail that is not colored in inside the tube. When the glue is dry, bend the tail into position.

Resting Lion

To make a lion having forty winks, make the body as for Lottie the lioness, but make a mane and face by following steps 5–11 on pages 13–14, drawing a sleepy face on the lion.

Treadgold the Tiger

The tiger growls and prowls about, and puts on quite an act,
but underneath that showing off, he's a great big pussy cat!

You will need

Toilet-paper tube, a narrow one
if possible

Approx. 4 x 4 in. (10 x 10 cm)
cereal-box cardboard

Head and paw templates (see
page 124)

General-purpose scissors

Tacky glue (see page 8)

Yellow and black paint

Paint brush

Ruler

Pencil

Paperclips

Black felt-tip pen

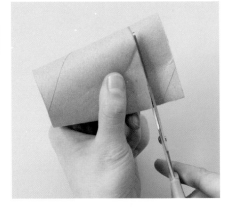

1 Measure 3 in. (8 cm) from the top of the toilet-paper tube and mark the point with a pencil. Draw a line all the way around, squeeze this end of the tube, and cut along the line.

2 Still pressing the sides of the tube together, cut off the corners at an angle.

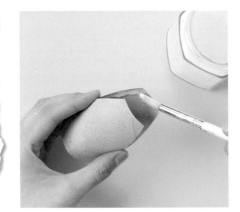

3 Glue the two sides of the tube together well using tacky glue.

4 Use the paperclips to hold the sides together while the glue dries. This will be the tiger's body.

5 When the glue is dry, remove the paperclips. Paint the body and the cereal-box cardboard yellow and leave to dry.

6 Position the tiger's head and paw templates (for the head, use the lioness head template on page 124) on the cardboard and draw around them with a pencil. You will need to make two paws. Cut these out. Also cut out a thin strip of cardboard to use as a tail.

7 Use a pencil to draw an outline for the stripes on the head and body, then paint or color them in black. Remember to do the back too! When that's dry, use the black felt-tip pen to draw a face on the head and claws on the paws.

8 Glue the head and two paws to the body with tacky glue and stick one end of the tail inside the body. When the glue is dry, bend the tail into position.

TIP
Why not paint spots instead of stripes to make a leopard or a cheetah? Use orange paint, rather than yellow.

Zany Zebras

Stripes are in this season and the zebras are delighted.
They're holding a zoo fashion show and everyone's invited!

You will need

2 toilet-paper tubes

Approx. 4 x 6 in. (10 x 15 cm)
cereal-box cardboard

Sheet of newspaper

Head template (see page 125)

Small scissors (see page 8)

General-purpose scissors

Glue

White and black paint

Paint brush

Ruler

Pencil

Spoon

Black felt-tip pen

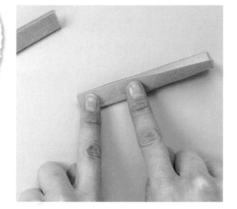

1 Using scissors, cut one of the tubes in half lengthwise and then cut two strips, each 1 in. (3cm) wide, from the tube pieces. Fold them in half lengthwise to make the legs.

2 On the other tube, measure 3½ in. (9 cm) from the top and mark with a pencil. Squeeze the end of the tube nearest the mark and cut across the tube.

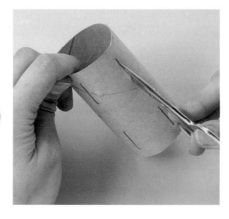

3 Hold the ruler along the tube and draw two lines, both ¾ in. (2 cm) long, about ½ in. (1 cm) in from each end. Repeat this 1 in. (3 cm) further around the tube, so the leg slots line up. Keeping the small scissors closed, place the point at the end of one of the lines, and press down, carefully twisting the scissors back and forth. Once you've made a hole, cut along the line, making sure the slots are big enough for the leg pieces.

4 Use the end of a spoon to wiggle in and out of the holes. This will make it easier to thread each leg through.

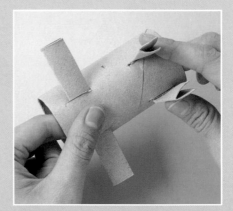

5 Thread the legs through. When they look level, fold them inward. Trim them to a length that looks right and keeps the body steady when it is turned over to stand on its legs.

TIP
Once the paint has soaked in, prop the body upside-down in an egg-carton lid to dry out completely—this stops the legs drying in a splayed-out fashion!

6 Paint the body and the cereal-box cardboard white. If you want to paint the zebra head on both sides, see page 9. When that's dry, use the head template to draw a head on the cardboard. Use the scissors to cut this out. Also cut a thin strip of cardboard for a tail.

7 Use a pencil to draw an outline for the mane and stripes on the head and body, before painting or coloring them in black. When that's dry, draw a face with the black felt-tip pen and color the tip of the tail. Glue the other end of the tail inside the body.

8 Snip carefully along the mane. Only cut into the black part of the mane.

9 Using a pencil, draw a line about ½ in. (1 cm) in from the head end of the body, long enough for the head tab to fit through. Use the small scissors to make a hole and cut a slot. Wiggle the scissors in and out to open it up a bit. Feed the tab of the head through.

10 Carefully push small, scrunched-up pieces of newspaper into the body on either side of the tab, to hold the head steady.

Terribly Tall Terry

Hiding is quite tricky when you're over 12 feet high, but it does make finding easy and is brilliant for "I Spy!"

You will need

2 toilet-paper tubes

Approx. 4 x 8 in. (10 x 20 cm) cereal-box cardboard

Sheet of newspaper

Head template (see page 126)

Small scissors (see page 8)

General-purpose scissors

Glue

Yellow and brown paint

Paint brush

Ruler

Pencil

Spoon

Fine black felt-tip pen

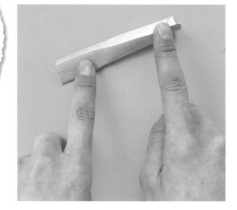

1 Using scissors, cut one of the tubes in half lengthwise and then cut two strips, each 1 in. (3 cm) wide, from the tube pieces. Fold them in half lengthwise to make the legs.

2 On the other tube, measure 3½ in. (9 cm) from the top and mark with a pencil. Squeeze the end of the tube nearest the mark and cut across the tube.

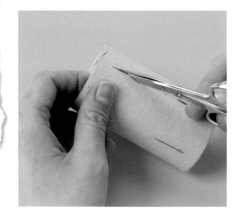

3 Hold the ruler along the tube and draw two lines, both ¾ in. (2 cm) long, about ½ in. (1 cm) in from each end. Repeat this 1 in. (3 cm) farther around the tube, so the leg slots line up. Keeping the small scissors closed, place the point at the end of one of the lines, and press down, carefully twisting the scissors back and forth. Once you've made a hole, cut along the line, making sure the slots are big enough for the leg pieces.

4 Use the end of a spoon to wiggle in and out of the holes. This will make it easier to thread each leg through the holes.

5 Thread the legs through. When they look level, fold them inward. Trim them to a length that looks right and keeps the body steady when it is turned over to stand on its legs.

6 Paint the body and the cereal-box cardboard yellow (see page 9 for painting both sides of the giraffe's head). When dry, use the template to cut out the head.

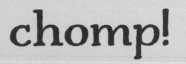

chomp!

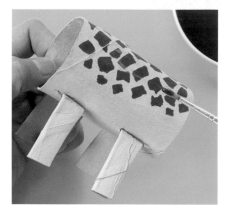

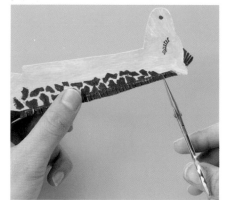

TIP
An egg-carton lid makes a great drying rack for card painted on both sides. Simply cut long slots on top of the lid and push the pieces in.

7 Use a pencil to draw an outline for the mane and spots on the head and body, before painting or coloring them in brown. When they are dry, draw a face with the black felt-tip pen and color the tip of the tail. Glue the other end of the tail inside the body.

8 Snip carefully along the mane. Only cut into the brown part of the mane.

9 Draw a slot long enough for the head tab, about ½ in. (1 cm) in from the end, then use the small scissors to pierce through the cardboard. Keep them closed, press down, and twist slightly until the point goes through the cardboard. Cut along the line and push the head into place.

10 Carefully push small, scrunched-up pieces of newspaper into the body on either side of the tab, to hold the head steady. Push a small ball of newspaper into the tail end of the tube, to stop the giraffe tipping forward.

Ellie the Elephant

Ellie adores gardening and tending to the flowers.
She waters daisies with her trunk and weeds for hours and hours.

This project starts with the head as this will help you choose a toilet-paper tube with the best diameter to fit the head (see the Tip box).

Egg carton

2 toilet-paper tubes

Approx. 4 x 6 in. (10 x 15 cm) cereal-box cardboard

Sheet of newspaper

Trunk and ear templates (see page 124)

Small scissors (see page 8)

General-purpose scissors

Tacky glue (see page 8)

Gray paint

Paint brush

Ruler

Pencil

Spoon

Black felt-tip pen

1 Using scissors, roughly cut out a whole cup from the end of an egg carton. An end cup is best, because there's more cardboard here so you can cut a shape that curves up a little at one side. This will be the head.

2 Squeeze the head into the end of one of the toilet-paper tubes, with the longer side tilted forward, until it feels wedged in (see the Tip box).

TIP
Try a few different-sized tubes. If you find the head is too big to fit, keep cutting carefully around the edge, following the curved shape, until it fits snugly.

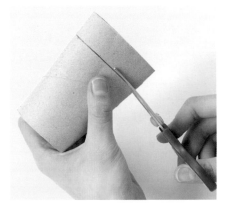

3 Take the head out. Measure 3 in. (8 cm) from the top of the tube and mark with a pencil. Squeeze the end of the tube nearest the mark and use scissors to cut across the tube.

4 Cut the other tube in half lengthwise and then cut two strips, each 1½ in. (4 cm) wide, from the tube pieces. Fold them in half lengthwise to make the legs.

5 Hold the ruler along the tube and draw two lines, both 1 in. (3 cm) long, about ½ in. (1 cm) in from each end. Repeat this 1 in. (3 cm) farther around the tube, so the leg slots line up. Keeping the small scissors closed, place the point at the end of one of the lines, and press down, carefully twisting the scissors back and forth. Once you've made a hole, cut along the line, making sure the slots are big enough for the leg pieces.

6 Use the end of a spoon to wiggle in and out of the holes. This will make it easier to thread each leg through. Thread the legs through. When they look level, fold them inward. Trim them to a length that looks right and keeps the body steady when it is turned over to stand on its legs.

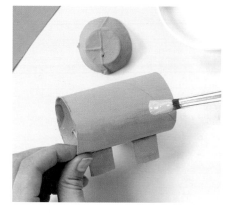

7 Paint the body, head, and the cereal-box cardboard gray (see page 9 if you want to paint both sides of the trunk).

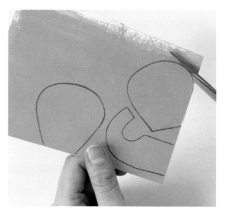

8 Once the paint is dry, position the templates on the cardboard and draw round them with a pencil. Cut them out. Also cut a thin strip of cardboard for a tail.

9 Put the head back into the end of the body, and use a pencil to draw a line down the middle. This will be where the trunk goes, so make sure it is long enough for the tab to fit. Then, take head out again. Carefully push the point of the small scissors through the cardboard, pressing and twisting, and cut along the line. Insert the trunk before replacing the head in the body.

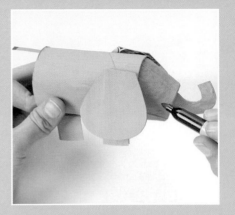

10 Using very tacky glue, stick the ears either side of the body by the head. It helps if you bend the ears so they are curved like the body, before gluing. Use a black felt-tip pen to draw eyes and to color in the tip of the tail. Glue the other end of the tail inside the body.

11 Scrunch up a piece of newspaper and push it in the tail end to give the elephant more stability.

Hetty the Happy Hippo

Hetty likes a mud bath,
she says mud is just the thing.
It's perfect sun protection and
does wonders for the skin.

You will need

Egg carton

2 toilet-paper tubes

Sheet of newspaper

Spoon

Snout, ear, and eye templates
(see page 123)

Small scissors (see page 8)

General-purpose scissors

Tacky glue (see page 8)

Orange-brown paint

Paint brush

Ball of modeling clay

Ruler

Pencil

Black felt-tip pen

squelch!

This project starts with the head as this will help you choose a toilet-paper tube with the best diameter to fit the head (see the Tip on page 27).

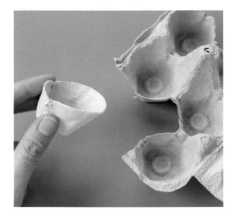

1 Using scissors, roughly cut out a whole cup from the end of an egg carton. An end cup is best, because there is more cardboard here, so you can cut a shape that curves up a little at one side. This will be the head.

2 Squeeze the head into the end of one of the toilet-paper tubes, with the longer side tilted forward, until it feels wedged in (see the Tip on page 27).

3 Take the head out. Measure 3 in. (8 cm) from the top of the tube and mark with a pencil. Squeeze the end of the tube nearest the mark and use scissors to cut across the tube.

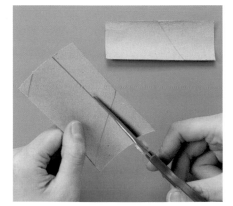

4 Cut the other tube in half lengthwise and then cut two strips, each 1½ in. (4 cm) wide, from the tube pieces. Fold them in half lengthwise to make the legs.

5 Hold the ruler along the tube and draw two lines, both 1 in. (3 cm) long, about ½ in. (1 cm) in from each end. Repeat this 1 in. (3 cm) farther around the tube, so the leg slots line up. Keeping the small scissors closed, place the point at the end of one of the lines, and press down, carefully twisting the scissors back and forth. Once you've made a hole, cut along the line, making sure the slots are big enough for the leg pieces.

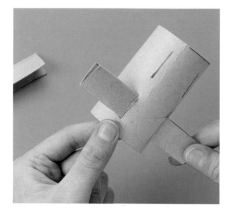

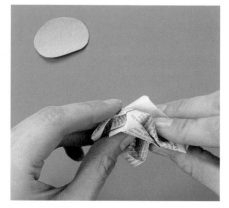

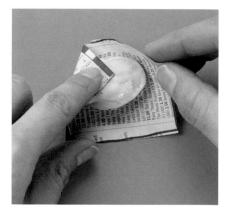

6 Use the end of a spoon to wiggle in and out of the holes. This will make it easier to thread each leg through. Thread the legs through. When they look level, fold them inward. Trim them to a length that looks right and keeps the body steady when it is turned over to stand on its legs.

7 Using the template on page 123, draw the hippo's snout on a piece of the leftover toilet-paper tube from Step 4. Cut this out. Cut a small piece of newspaper about 4 x 4 in. (10 x 10 cm) and scrunch it up until it fits on the snout piece. Glue it into place. It doesn't have to be neat.

8 Set the snout on some newspaper and draw around it, giving yourself a good margin for wrapping. Cut this out. Keeping the snout in the middle of the newspaper piece, turn the snout over so the lumpy bit is underneath, brush some glue on the card, and, tuck, wrap, and stick the newspaper around the snout.

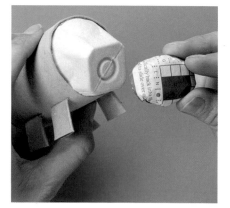

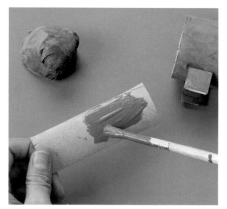

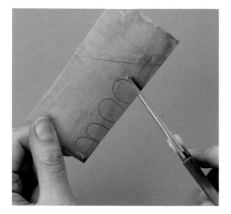

9 Glue the snout onto the hippo's head, then take the head out while the glue dries.

10 When the glue is dry, paint the hippo's body, head, and one of the strips of toilet-paper tube left over from Step 4.

11 When the paint is dry, use the templates to draw ears and eyes on the toilet-paper tube. Cut these out, as well as a thin strip for the tail.

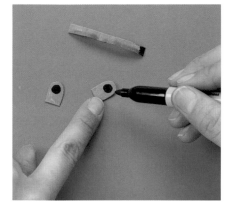

12 With black felt-tip pen, draw a black dot near the rounded end of the eyes and a black tip on the end of the tail. Glue the tail in place.

13 Put the head back in the tube and, near the join with the body, use a pencil to mark slots the right size for the ears and, in front of these, two more for the eyes.

14 Take the head out of the tube and put a small ball of modeling clay under to hold it steady. Then use the small scissors to push through the pencil marks on the card. Cut along the slots carefully. Wiggle the scissors in and out a bit, as this will make it easier to feed the ears and eyes through.

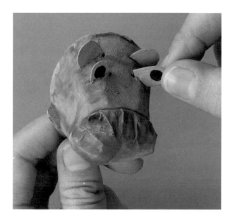

15 Slot the ears and eyes into position.

16 With black felt-tip pen, draw nostrils and a mouth on the snout. Put the head back into the tube.

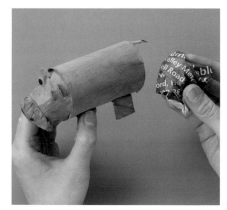
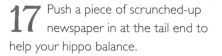

17 Push a piece of scrunched-up newspaper in at the tail end to help your hippo balance.

Rude Rhudie the Rhino

Rhudie's never happy, he's always in a mood.
It doesn't matter what you say, he's bound to be quite rude!

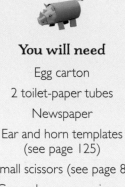

You will need

Egg carton

2 toilet-paper tubes

Newspaper

Ear and horn templates
(see page 125)

Small scissors (see page 8)

General-purpose scissors

Watered-down glue
(see page 8)

Tacky glue (see page 8)

Gray paint

Paint brush

Ruler

Pencil

Ball of modeling clay

Black felt-tip pen

This project starts with the head as this will help you choose a toilet-paper tube with the best diameter to fit the head (see the Tip box on page 27).

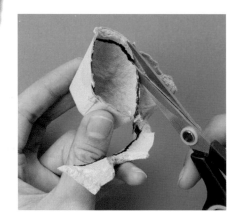

1 Using scissors, roughly cut out a whole cup from the end of an egg carton. An end cup is best, because there's more cardboard here, so you can cut a shape that curves up a little at one side. This will be the head.

2 Squeeze the head into the end of one of the toilet-paper tubes, with the longer side tilted forward, until it feels wedged in (see the Tip on page 27).

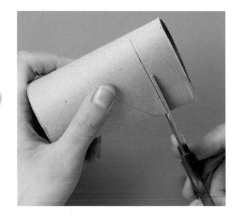

3 Take the head out. Measure 3 in. (8 cm) from the top of the tube and mark with a pencil. Squeeze the end of the tube nearest the mark and use scissors to cut across the tube.

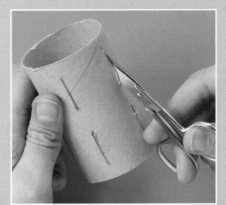

5 Hold the ruler along the tube and draw two lines, both 1 in. (3 cm) long, about ½ in. (1 cm) in from each end. Repeat this 1 in. (3 cm) farther around the tube, so the leg slots line up. Keeping the small scissors closed, place the point at the end of one of the lines, and press down, carefully twisting the scissors back and forth. Once you've made a hole, cut along the line, making sure the slots are big enough for the leg pieces.

4 Cut the other tube in half lengthwise and then cut two strips, each 1½ in. (4 cm) wide, from the tube pieces. Fold them in half lengthwise to make the legs.

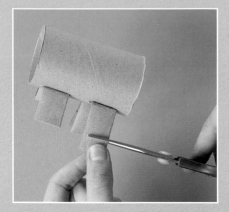  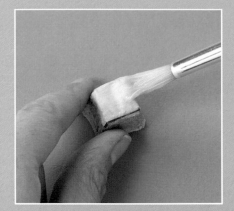

6 Use the end of a spoon to wiggle in and out of the holes. This will make it easier to thread each leg through. Thread the legs through. When they look level, fold them inward. Trim them to a length that looks right and keeps the body steady when it is turned over to stand on its legs.

7 Cut the top 1 in. (3 cm) off an egg carton cone, then draw a pencil mark around the middle of the cone. Gently squeeze the cone near the mark and cut straight across. The bottom half is going to be the rhino's snout.

8 Cut a piece of newspaper, just a little bigger than the end of the snout. Use watered-down glue to stick this in place so it covers the opening, brushing glue over the top of the newspaper as well, to really stick down the edges.

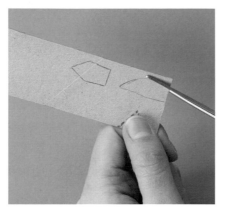
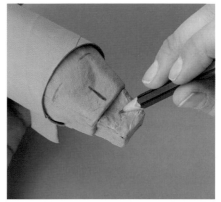

9 Use the tacky glue to glue the snout in place on the head, then take the head out while the glue dries.

10 When the glue is dry, paint the body, the head, and one of the strips of toilet-paper tube left over from step 4 gray on both sides. Leave another of the left-over strips unpainted.

11 Using the templates on page 125, draw two ears on the gray strip and two horns on the unpainted strip. Cut these out. Also cut a thin strip of the gray card to make a tail.

12 Put the head back into the tube and use a pencil to mark slots on the head to position the ears near the join with the body. Then mark two slots for the horns, near the end of the head for the smaller horn, and on the snout for the bigger one.

TIP
To speed things up, rather than covering the snout in step 8, fill the hole with a small, scrunched-up piece of newspaper. Also, instead of making slots for ears and horns, you can bend the tabs back and glue in place.

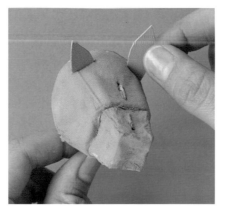
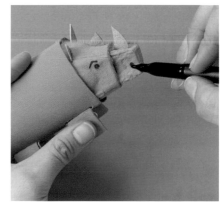

13 Take the head out of the tube and put a small ball of modeling clay under it to hold it steady. Then use the small scissors to push through the pencil marks on the card. Cut slots big enough for the ears and horns to fit. Wiggle the scissors in the holes to make it easier to push the ears and horns in. Insert the ears and horns.

14 Put the head back into the tube and glue the end of the tail inside the tube. Use a black felt-tip pen to draw hooded eyes and nostrils on the rhino's head. Push a piece of scrunched-up newspaper in at the tail end to help your rhino balance.

Fabulous Flamingos!

Flamingos flock together to catch up on the news.
They're like a fluffy sea of pink in a bay of blue.

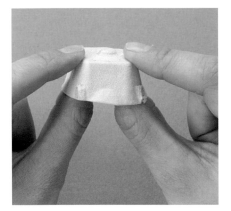

1 To make the flamingo body, use the scissors to cut out an egg cup from the egg carton. Push the bottom up a bit with your thumbs, to round it and make it more dome-shaped.

2 Rub down the shiny side of the cereal-box cardboard with sandpaper (see page 9) or you can use an egg-carton lid. Paint both sides of the cereal-box cardboard or egg-carton lid and the egg cup pink. They may need more than one coat. Leave to dry.

You will need

Egg carton

4 x 2 in. (10 x 5 cm) cereal-box cardboard or egg-carton lid

2 pink feathers

Orange or pink pipe cleaner, approx. 8 in. (20 cm)

Blue, light blue or white, yellow, and green paper

Ice-cream carton lid

Head template
(see page 124)

Small scissors (see page 8)

General-purpose scissors

Sandpaper

Glue and glue stick

Clear adhesive tape

Pink paint

Paint brush

Ruler

Small ball of modeling clay

Black felt-tip pen

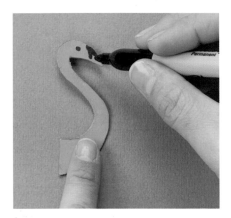

3 When the cardboard is dry, position the curvy head template on it, and draw round it with a pencil. Cut it out. Add eyes and a beak to the head with the black pen.

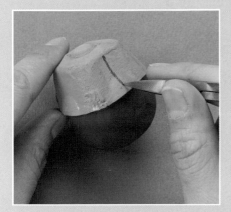

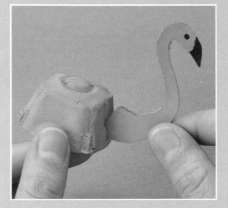

4 Use a pencil to draw a line down the middle of one egg cup side, long enough to fit the bottom of the neck, then use small scissors to pierce through the card (keep them closed, press, and twist). Put a ball of modeling clay under the egg cup, so there's something to push against. Remove the clay and cut along the line.

5 Carefully slot the head into the slit in the body.

6 Glue pink feathers either side and leave to dry.

squawk!

7 To make the legs, fold the pipe cleaner in half, and attach under the body with clear adhesive tape.

8 To make the pool for the flamingo to stand in, place the ice-cream carton lid on the piece of blue paper and draw around it.

9 Cut this out, then set it on top of the lid and press into the edges, all the way around, pushing the extra paper up the sides. Remove and cut along this crease line. Check the paper now fits neatly inside the lid, and trim a little more if you need to.

10 Place the blue cut-out shape on to the yellow and light blue (or white) paper, draw around it, and cut out both shapes.

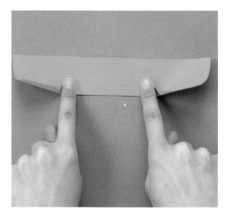

11 Measure and cut a 2 in. (5 cm) wide strip of green paper long enough to go round about a third of the lid edge (or as much as you'd like). Fold up the bottom ½ in. (1 cm).

12 Then use the scissors to snip a zigzag fringe of rushes, up to the fold. Experiment with different heights and widths. Uneven is best!

13 Cut the rushes strip into several sections so that it is easier to glue to the corners and around curves. Glue the folded edge to the lid.

14 To make the beach, cut the yellow piece of paper in half, and glue down on the lid at the opposite end to the rushes.

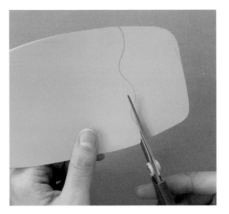

15 Draw and cut a wavy line about a quarter of the way along the blue paper. Place this on the light blue (or white) paper shape and copy a few wavy lines, about ½ in. (1 cm) wide. Cut these out.

16 Stick the blue paper onto the lid and position the waves to look like they're breaking on the beach. Glue into place.

17 Cut a small circle out of the spare light blue (or white) paper and a slightly smaller circle out of the blue paper and place them, one on top of the other, where you want your flamingo to stand (you can paint these circles and the waves on if you prefer).

18 Use small scissors to pierce a very small hole in the middle of the circles (best done by an adult as the plastic lid may be tough), and push about 1 in. (3 cm) of one of the pipe cleaner legs through. Bend this under the lid and stick in place with clear adhesive tape.

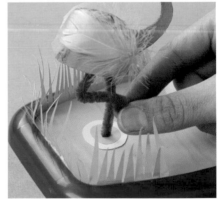

19 Cut the other leg so that it is a similar length and bend the sharp end over. Strike a flamingo pose! If you like, cut out small yellow rectangles from the yellow paper and stick them to the ends of some of the rushes.

jungle

Welcome to the Jungle!
Keep your eyes up please!
There are lots of cheeky monkeys
Hiding in the trees.

Cheeky Chimps

The chimps just love to mess about, and some can be quite bad.
They chuck bananas, make a din, and drive the others mad!

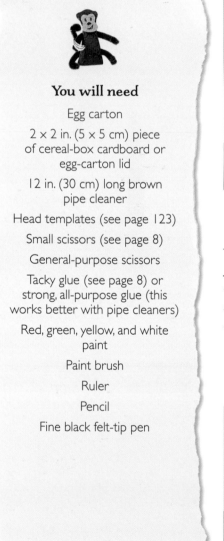

You will need

Egg carton

2 x 2 in. (5 x 5 cm) piece of cereal-box cardboard or egg-carton lid

12 in. (30 cm) long brown pipe cleaner

Head templates (see page 123)

Small scissors (see page 8)

General-purpose scissors

Tacky glue (see page 8) or strong, all-purpose glue (this works better with pipe cleaners)

Red, green, yellow, and white paint

Paint brush

Ruler

Pencil

Fine black felt-tip pen

1 Roughly cut out a whole egg-carton cone. Measure 1 in. (3 cm) from the top and mark dots around the cone. Join these dots with a pencil line and cut up from the bottom of the cone and along the line. This will be the chimp's body.

2 Paint this and half the piece of cereal-box cardboard or egg-carton cardboard brown. (For brown, mix a small amount of red paint with some green until you have a rich chocolate color.) Paint the other half pale brown (to get pale brown, add a dab of brown paint to yellow and white paint). Leave to dry.

3 Use the template to draw the larger head piece on the brown cardboard and the smaller head piece on the pale brown cardboard.

4 Carefully cut them out with small scissors. Glue the pale brown piece to the brown piece and leave to dry.

5 While that's drying, use the small scissors to make holes either side of the body—two about ¼ in. (5 mm) from the top for the arms and two about ½ in. (1 cm) from the bottom for the legs. Keep the scissors closed, press down on the cardboard, and twist to and fro. Make another hole at the very top for the head and cut a ½ in. (1 cm) groove at the back for the tail.

6 Cut the pipe cleaner into three pieces, one 5 in. (12 cm long) and two 3½ in. (9 cm) long. Push the longer one down through the head hole, until about 1 in. (3 cm) is left sticking out the top. Bend this bit into a small loop. Pull the tail part up through the groove.

7 Push the other two pieces of pipe cleaner through the arm and leg holes, remembering to bend all the sharp tips over.

8 Draw a face with black felt-tip pen (try different expressions).

9 Stick the head onto the pipe-cleaner loop with a generous blob of tacky or all-purpose glue.

Bobby the Baboon

For the baboon, make a chimp body, following the steps on pages 44–46, but use the head templates on page 123. Remember to add a red rear end!

Use the templates to copy the little pieces for the face onto some cereal-box or egg carton cardboard. Cut them out carefully with small scissors (good scissor practice as it is quite fiddly!). Use yellow, brown, blue, and red felt-tip pens or pencils to color in the pieces. Glue the little pieces together: brown face on to the mane, then the blue bit, followed by the red nose. Dot on some yellow paint for eyes. Leave to dry, then draw on eye dots and nostrils with a black felt-tip pen. Glue the head on to the body.

Ozzy the Orangutan

Orangutan, Orangutan, swinging through the trees, Orangutan, Orangutan, makes it look a breeze!

You will need

Egg carton

3 x 3 in. (8 x 8 cm) piece of cereal-box cardboard or egg-carton lid

Arm and leg template (see page 123)

Small scissors (see page 8)

General-purpose scissors

Tacky glue (see page 8)

Red, yellow, blue, and white paint

Paint brush

Small ball of modeling clay

Ruler

Pencil

Fine black felt-tip pen

As well as the obvious shapes you find in an egg carton, there are some other bits that are brilliant for making creatures. One favorite is the little cardboard catch that keeps the carton shut. If they're round (rather than pointy), they're perfect for making a very quick and easy orangutan face. If your carton doesn't have rounded catches, a chimp head without the ears (see template on page 123) will work fine instead.

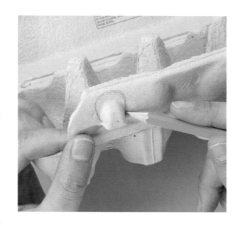

1 Draw around the egg-carton catch with a pencil, allowing a bit extra for the top of the head, and cut this out.

2 Roughly cut out an egg-carton cone. Measure 1½ in. (4 cm) from the top of the cone, mark a line all around the cone for guidance, and cut out. This will be the orangutan's body. Paint this, the top of the head, and both sides of the cereal-box cardboard or egg-carton lid orangey-brown (mix red and yellow paint, then gradually add a little blue paint to get the right shade). Leave to dry.

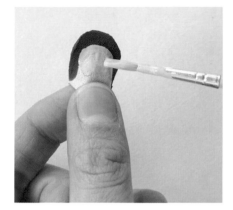

3 Paint the rounded part of the head pale orange (mix some white paint with a little of the orangey-brown to get this color). Leave to dry.

4 Use the template to draw two arms and two legs on the cereal-box cardboard or egg carton lid. Cut them out.

5 About ½ in. (1 cm) from the bottom of the body, draw slots that slope forward and down, long enough for the leg tabs . About ½ in. (1 cm) from the top of the body, on one side draw a slot for an arm, sloping at the same angle as the leg. Make the other arm slot a vertical line.

6 Use the small scissors to pierce through the cardboard on each line. To help make the leg slots, put a ball of modeling clay behind, so there is something to press against. Snip along the lines and wiggle the scissors in and out so that it is easier to get the tabs through. Push the limbs into place.

7 Draw eyes, nostrils, and a mouth with a fine black felt-tip pen and glue the head onto the body with tacky glue.

Gloria the Gorilla
You could also use these steps to make a gorilla! Just paint the body pieces black and the face gray. Why not cut a few banana shapes out of some yellow-painted cardboard, too?

Mr. Crocodile

Two beady eyes, a long, green snout,
a sinister, toothy smile...
Best to keep your distance
from Mr. Crocodile!

You will need

Egg carton
3 x 2 in. (8 x 5 cm) cereal-box cardboard
Toilet-paper tube
Small sheet of white paper
Templates (see page 123)
2 paperclips
Small scissors (see page 8)
General-purpose scissors
Tacky glue (see page 8)
Glue stick (optional)
Green and yellow paint
Paint brush
Ruler
Pencil
Fine black felt-tip pen

1 Cut the longest piece of cone you can from the middle of the egg carton. Make sure there are no bumpy joins on it. Then cut the cone in half lengthwise.

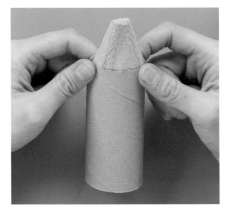

2 To make the croc's tail, flatten out the wide end of one cone half, and glue this just under one end of the toilet-paper tube, pressing it into the curve. Use paperclips to hold in place and leave it to dry.

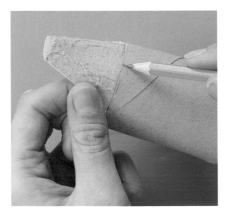

3 When it's dry, use a pencil to mark the mid-point of the tail on the tube. Using a ruler, draw a line from this point along the tube to the other end.

TIP

Small scissors are best for cutting the cone in half. Avoid a sticking-up tail by keeping the cone piece as level as possible with the tube when you glue it in place.

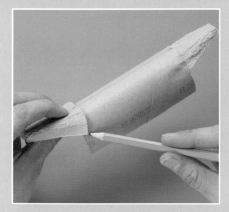  

4 Line up the pencil line on the tube with the middle of the other cone half. Hold the cone half in place on the end and, without flattening it, mark where the corners touch the tube on top.

5 Cut straight along the underside of the tube and flatten it out, also flattening the cone. Use a ruler to draw a line from the marks you made in step 4 to the end of the tail, on both sides, then cut along the lines. You will lose some of the tail cone when you are cutting.

6 Cut about ¾ in. (2 cm) from the head end, until the tube part of the body, excluding the cone, measures 3 in. (8 cm) long.

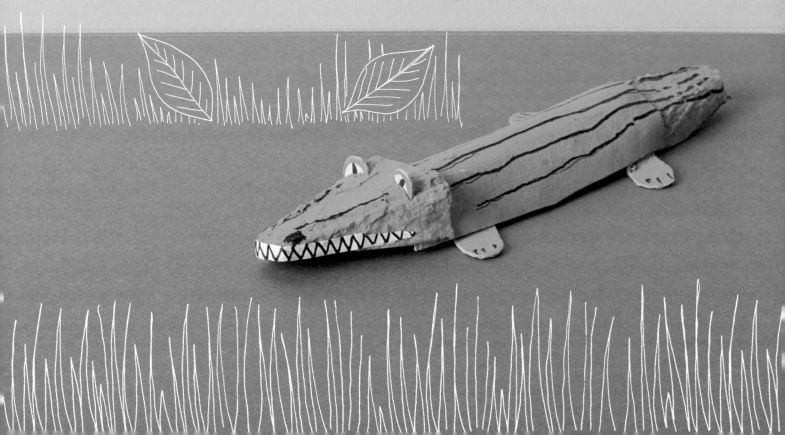

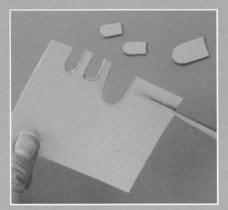

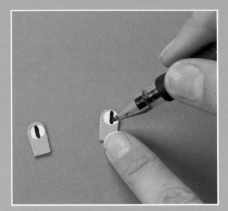

7 Paint the body, the head, and piece of cereal-box cardboard green, and leave to dry.

8 Use the templates to draw four feet (use the hippo ear template on page 123) and two eyes on to the green cardboard. Cut these out.

9 Add a thick dot of yellow paint near the rounded end of each eye. Leave to dry, then draw a line down the middle of each eye with a fine black felt-tip pen.

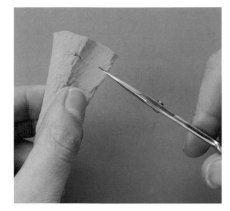

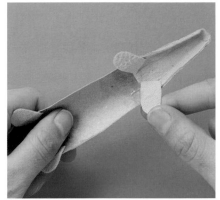

10 About ½ in. (1 cm) from the back of the head, mark two lines long enough for the eye tabs on the ridges. Carefully pinch a ridge together and use the small scissors to snip across each line. Wiggle the scissors in and out a bit to open up the gaps and thread the eye tabs through.

11 Squeeze the cardboard body back into its curved shape and stick the end of the head right on the end of it with tacky glue. The bottom edges of the head and the body should line up so your croc lies flat. Any unruly corners can be trimmed off later. Leave to dry. (If the gluing is proving tricky, use some clear adhesive tape underneath the body to hold the head in place.)

12 Glue the four feet underneath, angled forward. Leave the glue to dry, then carefully bend each foot into position.

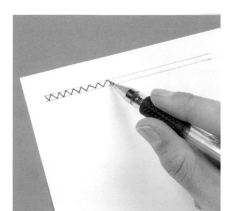

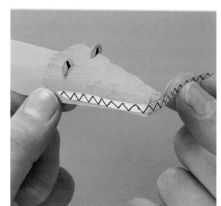

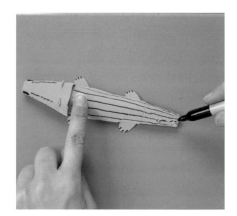

13 For the teeth, use the fine black felt-tip pen to draw two 4 in. (10 cm) parallel lines about ¼ in. (5 mm) apart on the white paper. Then zigzag with the black pen between the lines. Cut this strip out.

14 Wrap the teeth around the head, from just under one eye to the other. Cut away any bit you don't need and snip each end into a gradual point. Glue in place. You may find a glue stick easiest to do this.

15 Then draw on nostrils, two long lines along the snout, claws, and some line markings along the back with a black felt-tip pen.

Peter the Panda

Peter's such a happy soul who loves a bamboo shoot.
The only thing that makes him cross is when he is called "cute!"

You will need

Egg carton

6 x 2 in. (15 x 5 cm) cereal-box cardboard or an egg-carton lid

2 toothpicks

Green tissue paper

Ear template (see page 123)

Small scissors (see page 8)

General-purpose scissors

Tacky glue (see page 8)

White and black paint

Paint brush

Sandpaper

Small ball of modeling clay

Ruler

Pencil

Black felt-tip pen

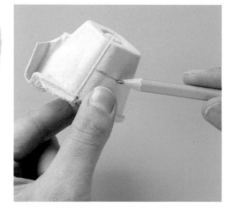

1 Roughly cut out two whole egg cups so they're easier to work with, then measure and mark ¾ in. (2 cm) points around each one. (Spending a little time measuring will make it easier to stick the cups together.) Join the points with a pencil line and cut carefully along the line.

2 To make the body, put the cups together and twist around until you get a good fit, trimming away bumpy bits. Mark each cup so you know which sides match up. Use tacky glue to stick them together and fill any gaps. Leave to dry.

3 To make the head, cut another egg cup from the carton. It's best if this one comes from one end of the carton, where there's more cardboard, so you can curve one side up into a lip or tab shape.

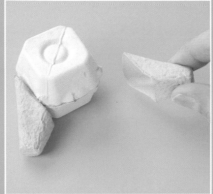

4 Roughly cut out two middle cones for legs. Then measure ¾ in. (2 cm) from the top on one side and draw a pencil line across. Do the same at the 1½ in. (4 cm) point on the opposite side, and join the lines. Cut the two cones out.

5 Place the cone legs against the body to see how they sit. Keep snipping until you're happy with the fit. Remember, it really doesn't have to be perfect, a few gaps won't stop the legs sticking to the body. Don't glue the legs on yet though.

6 Paint the body and head white. Paint the legs, plus both sides of the cereal-box cardboard (rub the shiny side with sandpaper first, see page 9) or the egg carton lid black. Leave to dry.

munch!

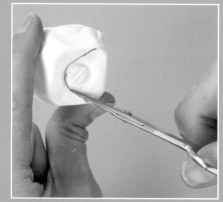

7 Draw a 4½ in. (11 cm) long arm piece (use the photo above as a guide) and two ears on the cardboard (for the ears, use the hippo ear template on page 123). Cut them out.

8 Draw a semi-circular slot on top of the egg cup body, from one side to the other, curving about ½ in. (1 cm) in from the front. Pierce through the cardboard with small scissors (keep closed, press, and twist), then carefully cut along the curve.

9 Push the head tab into the slot to check it fits. If it sticks out too much, make the head tab smaller. Once you're happy, take it out again.

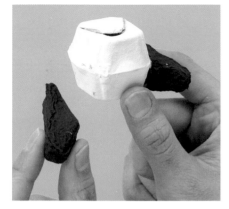

10 Stick the legs on to the body with plenty of tacky glue to fill any gaps.

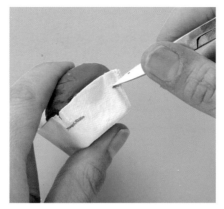

11 While that's drying, use a pencil to mark slots on top of the head, big enough for the ears. Put a ball of modeling clay behind the cardboard so there's something to push against. Make a hole with small scissors (keep closed, press, and twist). Cut along the lines and wiggle the scissors in and out to make it easier to feed the ears through.

12 Push the ears into the slots. Draw a face on the head with black felt-tip pen. Start the eyes by drawing a small circle—don't fill it in, but color around it.

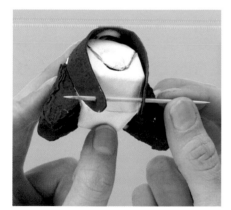

13 Take the arm piece and make a hole near each end with the small scissors. Glue this strip around the sides and back of the body. It should sit a little higher than the body at the back. Push a toothpick through the holes to hold the arms in place and leave until the glue dries.

14 To make a bamboo shoot, cut the pointy ends off the other toothpick, dab glue on one end, and wrap two 1 x 2 in. (3 x 5 cm) pieces of green tissue paper tightly around it. Snip the tissue paper to make a leafy top.

15 When the glue for the arms is dry, remove the toothpick holding them in place and carefully insert the bamboo shoot through the holes.

snow

They call themselves the "Ice Pack"
and what a happy bunch!
No one's ever frosty, and there's
always fish for lunch.

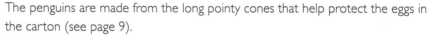

A Party of Penguins

The penguins are great singers, they love to entertain.
They'll perform in any weather and like singing in the rain!

The penguins are made from the long pointy cones that help protect the eggs in the carton (see page 9).

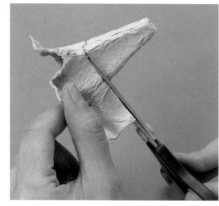

You will need

Egg carton

1 x 2 in. (3 x 5 cm) cereal-box cardboard

Small scissors (see page 8)

General-purpose scissors

Glue

Yellow, white, and black paint

Paint brush

Ruler

Pencil

Fine black felt-tip pen

1 Roughly cut out a whole cone from the egg carton so it's easier to work with. Measure 1½ in. (4 cm) from the top and mark each side. Join the marks with a pencil line and then cut up from the bottom of the cone and along the line. Spending a little time measuring will stop you ending up with a wobbly penguin! Make your penguin bigger or smaller if you want.

2 Paint one side of the cone with a thick coat of white paint. Paint the cereal-box cardboard yellow. Leave to dry.

3 Use the pencil to draw an outline on the white side of the cone for the penguin's chest and face. Then paint the rest of the cone black. When it's dry, dot on some eyes with a fine black felt-tip pen.

> **TIP**
> You can simply skip steps 4 and 5 and draw or paint on a beak instead.

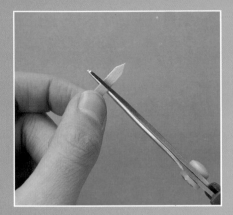

4 Cut a thin strip of yellow cardboard for the beak, snip one end into a "V" shape, and cut off about ½ in. (1 cm).

5 To position the beak, make a horizontal slot under the eyes with the small scissors (keep the scissors flat and closed, press down, and twist slightly until the point pokes through). Make sure it's wide enough for the beak. Put a dab of glue behind the slot and push the beak in.

6 Cut two small, thin triangles from the yellow cardboard for feet and round off the ends a little. Glue the pointy ends underneath the cone and leave to dry before bending into place.

A Splash of Seals

Arf! Arf! go the seals
as they laze on the snow.
In water they whizz,
but on land they're so slow.

You will need

Egg carton
Small scissors (see page 8)
Gray paint
Paint brush
Ruler
Pencil
Fine black felt-tip pen

1 Cut out as much of an egg-carton cone as you can, right down to the bottom. It doesn't have to be neat.

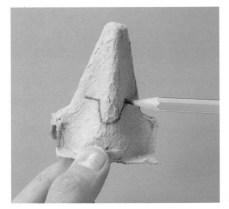

2 Choose which side you want for the front, and measure and draw a short horizontal line in the middle, 1 in. (3 cm) from the top of the cone. Mark points in the middle of the other sides, also 1 in. (3 cm) from the top of the cone.

3 To make the flippers, use the corners as a guide and draw down about ½ in. (1 cm) at a slope from the front line, and then up the next side to the mid-point. Repeat for the other flipper.

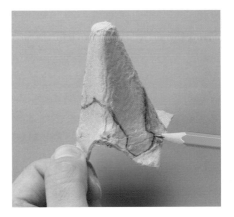

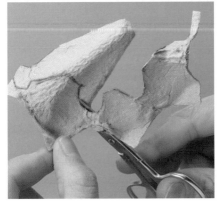

4 Draw across from the flipper to the corner on both sides. Then bring the two lines together at the back to form the tail, going as close to the bottom of the cone as you can.

5 Use the small scissors to cut out the shape, taking your time.

6 As the egg carton cardboard can be prone to ripping, snip across the top of the flippers at the front, going not quite as far as the corners.

7 Then carefully bend the flippers and the tail back.

8 Round off the pointy bits left from snipping the flippers at the front.

9 Paint the seal light gray and leave to dry.

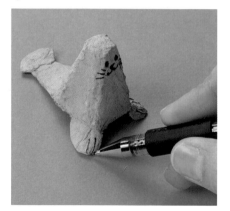

10 Then use the fine black felt-tip pen to draw the seal's face and a few lines on each flipper.

11 Why not make some fish for your seals? (See page 119.)

Walter the Walrus

To make a walrus, follow the steps for making a seal up to step 8, making the body just a little longer, if you can.

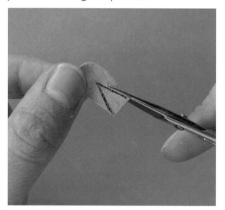

1 Copy the walrus snout and tusks template on page 125 onto a small piece of egg carton or cereal-box cardboard. Cut this out.

2 Paint the walrus body brown and the snout paler brown or orange-brown, and leave the tusks unpainted or paint them white. Using a fine black felt-tip pen, draw on the walrus nose, mouth, and dots for whiskers. Glue it on to the walrus body, and draw eyes above the snout.

Purdy the Polar Bear

She looks so very cuddly with her furry white coat, but the chance of a bear hug is really quite remote!

You will need

2 toilet-paper tubes

4 x 4 in. (10 x 10 cm) cereal-box cardboard (optional)

Egg carton (optional)

Sheet of newspaper

Head template (see page 124)

Small scissors (see page 8)

General-purpose scissors

Tacky glue (see page 8)

White paint

Paint brush

Spoon (optional)

Ruler

Pencil

Black felt-tip pen

The body is similar to the giraffe's (see page 24) and the zebra's (see page 21). Narrower tubes are best for the polar bear.

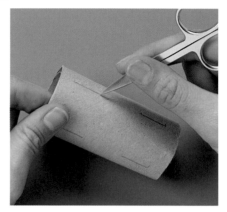

1 Cut one of the toilet-paper tubes in half lengthwise and then cut two strips, each 1 in. (3 cm) wide from the tube pieces. Fold them in half lengthwise to make the legs.

2 Cut about 1 in. (3cm) off the other tube, so you're left with a 3 in. (8 cm) long piece. To make the leg slots, hold a ruler along the tube and draw two lines, both ¾ in. (2 cm) long, about ½ in. (1 cm) in from each end. Repeat this 1 in. (3 cm) farther around the tube, so the leg slots line up.

3 Keep the small scissors closed and press the tip on the end of one of the lines near the middle of the tube. Push the scissors down and twist until the tip pokes through the cardboard. Cut along the line, making sure the slot is big enough for the leg piece. Cut the other three slots.

4 Thread the legs through, using the scissors or the end of a spoon to help open up the slot. Your polar bear needs to have short legs, so cut them until you're happy with the length, and the body is steady.

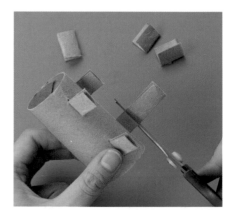

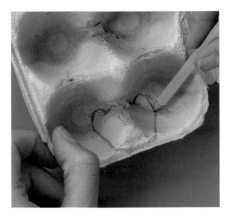

5 To make the head, you can either copy the template on to the cardboard or you can cut one from the inside of an egg carton. The molded part between the egg cups is perfect for a snout. Draw a head shape around the snout. The ears will end up in the bottom of the two egg cups, either side of the raised part.

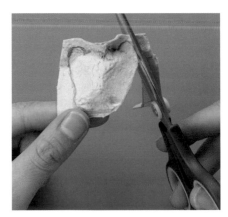

6 Cut this out roughly first, before neatening up and trimming if you need to.

7 Scrunch up a piece of newspaper to fit in one end of the tube body. Leave it sticking out slightly so that you can glue the head to it once it's painted.

8 Paint the body, head, and a small strip of cardboard for a tail. They may need a few coats. When dry, draw eyes, a nose, and a mouth on the head with a felt-tip pen, then glue the head and the tail in place.

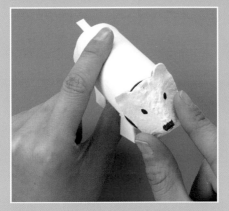

aviary

Busy, bright, and noisy,
you've found the Aviary!
Non-stop chirpy chatter,
it's a colorful jamboree!

Pretty Pesky Parrots

The parrots are great mimics but can be very loud.
They're excellent at ring-tone tunes and whistling at the crowd.

You will need

Egg carton

Wing and tail feather templates
(see page 124)

Small scissors (see page 8)

General-purpose scissors

Glue

Paints in all your favorite colors

Paint brush

Ruler

Pencil

Fine black felt-tip pen

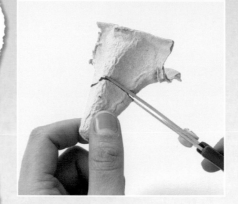

1 For the parrot's body, roughly cut out a whole cone from the egg carton, then measure 1 in. (3 cm) from the top and mark three sides. Join these marks with a pencil line, and on the remaining side draw a "V" about ¾ in. (2 cm) long. The "V" will be part of the tail feathers.

2 Cut out carefully and bend the tail feathers back.

3 Using the templates on page 124, draw wings and the under part of the tail feathers on the egg-carton lid (or a small sheet of spare cardboard) and cut them out.

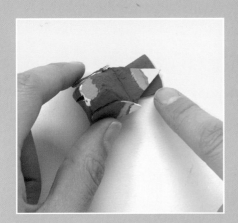

4 Now the really fun bit—painting your parrot! Copy a picture or make up your own colorful pattern. Anything goes! Paint the body, wings, and under part of the tail feathers.

5 While the paint is drying, cut a thin strip of cardboard for the beak and color both sides with a black felt-tip pen. Curve one end to make a hooked shape and snip off about ½ in. (1 cm). Mark a short vertical line near the top of the head for the beak and carefully pierce through the card with the small scissors. Keep the scissors closed and press down firmly, twisting slightly Make sure the hole is big enough for the beak.

6 Dab some glue behind the slot and feed the beak through. Use a fine black felt-tip pen to draw eyes either side of the beak, and glue the wings and the tail feathers in place.

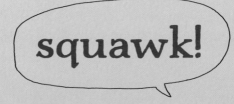

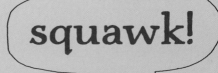

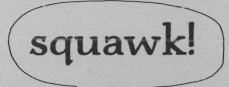

Birds of a Feather

The parrot shape on page 70 can be used to make a whole host of real and imaginary birds. You can make the body bigger or smaller, or make longer, more impressive tail feathers. Have fun decorating, too: why not use a gold pen for a bit of bling!

For both birds you will need

Egg carton

3 x 4 in. (8 x 10 cm) piece of cereal-box cardboard or an egg-carton lid (this will give the tail more texture)

Fantail template (see page 124)

Small scissors (see page 8)

General-purpose scissors

Glue

Green, blue, and yellow paint, plus the color of your choice for the lovebird

Paint brush

Paperclip

Ruler

Pencil

Colored felt-tip pens

Fine black felt-tip pen

For the peacock you will also need

Gold pen (optional)

For the lovebird you will also need

4 small colored feathers

Peacock

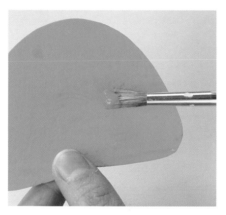

1 To make the body, roughly cut out a whole cone from the egg carton, then measure 1 in. (3 cm) from the top and mark three sides. Join these marks with a pencil line, and on the remaining side draw a "V" about ¾ in. (2 cm) long. (See step 1 on page 70.)

2 Use the template to draw the fantail on to the egg-carton lid or cereal-box cardboard. Cut this out and paint both sides green. Paint the body blue. Leave to dry.

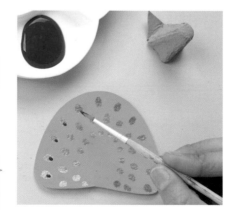

3 With a gold pen or yellow paint, draw spots spaced out evenly around the top of the tail. On the next row do the same, but placing them in between the spots above, and so on. Allow to dry, then dot some blue paint on to each gold or yellow spot.

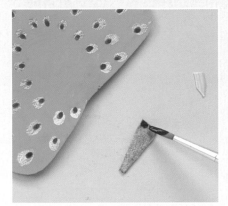
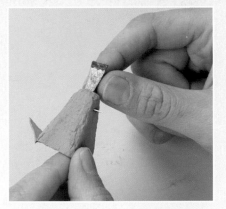
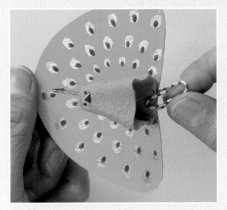

4 Cut a thin strip of cardboard for the beak and a small triangle shape for the head crest. Use a felt-tip pen to color the beak strip yellow, before snipping one end into a "V" shape. Cut off about ½ in. (1 cm). Color the head crest gold or yellow, and finish with a line of blue. Dot on some eyes near the top of the cone body with a fine black felt-tip pen.

5 Use the small scissors to pierce a horizontal hole for the beak under the eyes, and one on top of the head for the crest. Alternatively, you can fold over the pointy end of the crest and glue into position. Push both pieces into place.

6 Bend and glue the "V" shape at the back of the body to the body, then glue on the fantail. Use a paperclip to hold it secure while the glue dries.

TIP
For speed, you can simply paint on a beak, if you like, for any of the birds in this chapter.

Lovebird

The feathered lovebird is really easy!

1 To make the body, cut the top 1 in. (3 cm) from an egg-carton cone and paint it any color you like, to complement the feathers. When it's dry, dot on eyes near the top of the cone with a fine black felt-tip pen.

2 Cut a thin strip of cardboard for the beak and color it yellow with a felt-tip pen. Snip one end into a "V" shape and cut off about ½ in. (1 cm).

3 Use the small scissors to pierce a horizontal hole under the eyes for the pointy beak, one on top for the feather crest, and another at the back, near the bottom, for the tail plume.

4 Dab some glue behind the holes. Push the beak, feather crest, and tail plume into place.

5 Glue the remaining two wing feathers on either side. Trim the feathers if you need to.

Flying Parrots

They swoop and they swirl, soaring up high,
a rainbow of colors, up in the sky.

You will need

Egg carton

4 x 4 in. (10 x 10 cm) cereal-box
cardboard or egg-carton lid

Tail feather template
(see page 124)

Small scissors (see page 8)

General-purpose scissors

Glue

Paint in a variety of colors

Paint brush

Needle

Approx. 20 in. (50 cm) white
thread

Pencil

Fine black felt-tip pen

If you've already visited the aquarium on page 83, then these may look familiar! That's because the flying parrots come from the sides of an egg carton, like the stingray and manta ray. The curves of the egg cups are perfect for the wings, and the raised, molded part in the middle forms the body. You should find this shape along any side of an egg carton. I've drawn two below, with wings up, to show you.

1 Use a pencil to sketch a flying bird shape in the carton and roughly cut around it.

2 To make a parrot with its wings down, simply turn the parrot template upside down. Two for the price of one!

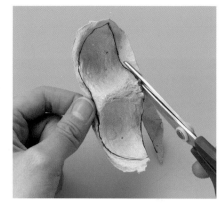

3 Go over the outline carefully with the pencil and cut the shape out. Decide whether you want the wings to be up or down.

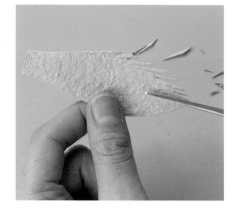

4 Copy the tail feather template onto the cereal-box cardboard or egg carton lid. Cut it out. Cut long zigzags into it if you want, for a feathery effect. You can do the same to the wings too.

5 Glue the tail feathers in place— underneath if your parrot has its wings up, or on top if the wings are pointing down.

6 Painting time! Make your parrots as colorful as possible. Remember to paint underneath too.

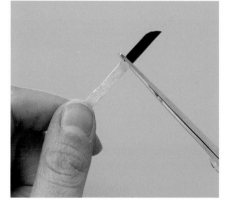

7 Cut a thin strip of cereal-box cardboard, then color both sides with black felt-tip pen. Curve one end to make a hooked beak shape and cut off no more than ½ in. (1 cm).

8 Mark a small vertical line on the bird's face with the pencil, for the beak, and very carefully pierce a hole here with the small scissors (keep closed, press, and twist a little; don't push too hard!). Make sure the slot is big enough for the beak.

9 Put a dab of glue behind the head for the "wings-up" parrot, or just a little on the end of the beak tab for the "wings-down" one, and push the beak into place. If it is catching on the tail feathers, shorten the tab. Dot on eyes with the fine black felt-tip pen.

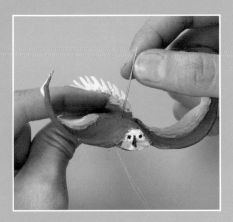

10 Thread the needle and tie a good knot at the end of the thread. Push the needle up through the middle of the body. Don't worry too much if the parrots tilt up or down— it's good to have them flying in different directions!

Hunter the Eagle

"Old Eagle Eyes," they call him, and he doesn't miss a trick... Though once he caught a grass snake that turned out to be a stick!

The eagle is very similar to the flying parrot (see page 75) with "wings down." It can come from any side of the egg carton too.

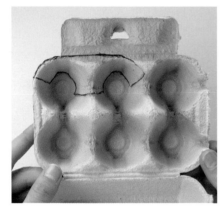

1 Sketch the eagle shape inside the carton. The ends of the eagle's wings go straight across the sides of the egg cups. Follow the curve at the bottom of the egg cups for the back of the wings.

2 Keep as much of the join with a middle cone as you can too; this will be the eagle's claws.

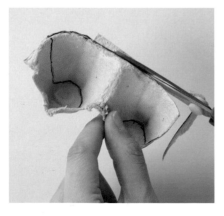

3 Cut around your shape roughly first. Then go over the outline with the pencil and cut out carefully. Remember to keep the cardboard join.

You will need

Egg carton

4 × 4 in. (10 × 10 cm) cereal-box cardboard or egg-carton lid

Tail feathers template (see page 123)

Small scissors (see page 8)

General-purpose scissors

Glue

White, brown, and orange paint

Paint brush

Pencil

Fine black felt-tip pen

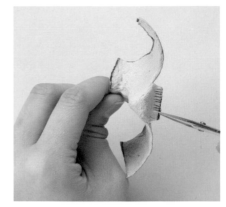

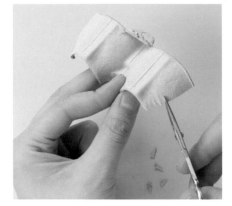

4 Like the flying parrots, the card join between the cups forms the head. Make the head plumage more prominent by cutting the side bits away and snipping into the card. Small scissors are best for this.

5 Copy the tail feathers template on to the cereal-box cardboard or egg-carton lid. Cut the tail feathers out. Snip zigzags to make the tail feathers look more feathery and ragged, and do the same to the wing ends.

6 Glue the tail feathers in place on top and leave to dry. Paint the wings and the back of the body brown. Allow to dry and then paint the head and end of the tail feathers white. Paint underneath too.

TIP
You can skip steps 8 and 9 and paint a beak on instead.

7 Paint the claws orange, as well as both sides of some spare cardboard.

8 Cut a thin strip from the orange cardboard and curve one end to make a hooked beak shape. Cut off about ½ in. (1 cm).

9 Mark a small vertical line on the head and carefully pierce a hole through the cardboard with small scissors (keep closed, press, and twist a little; don't push too hard!). Dab some glue on the tab end, and push the beak in. Trim if it is catching on the tail feathers.

10 Dot eyes either side with a fine black felt-tip pen. Shape the claws more if you want to. If you want to make a rock for your eagle to perch on, see page 111 for instructions.

aquarium

A watery world of wonder,
all kinds of sealife here—
Turtles, dolphins, stingrays,
and a shark they don't go near!

Dashing Dolphins

Dolphins are so friendly and love to play all day,
but when they race around the rocks it's best to clear the way!

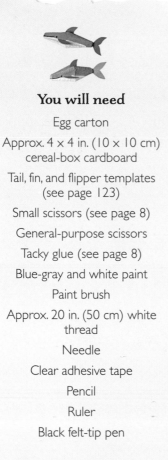

You will need

Egg carton

Approx. 4 x 4 in. (10 x 10 cm)
cereal-box cardboard

Tail, fin, and flipper templates
(see page 123)

Small scissors (see page 8)

General-purpose scissors

Tacky glue (see page 8)

Blue-gray and white paint

Paint brush

Approx. 20 in. (50 cm) white
thread

Needle

Clear adhesive tape

Pencil

Ruler

Black felt-tip pen

The dolphin is made from two egg-box cones stuck together—the tricky part is doing this without too many gaps around the join (though a few are fine!). The best way to get a good fit is to spend time measuring.

1 Using scissors, roughly cut out two whole cones from the egg carton—this makes them easier to work with.

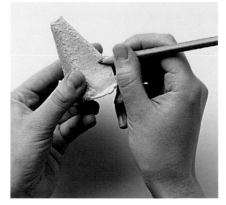

2 Using a pencil, make a mark on the cone just above the point where the join was in the egg carton.

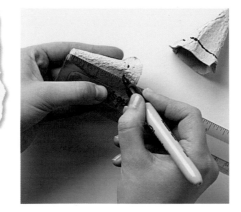

3 Using a ruler, check the measurement from the top of the cone, then use this to measure and mark all the sides and corners on both cones. Join the marks by drawing a line.

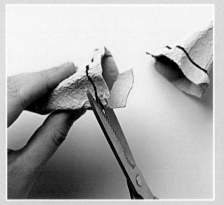

4 Carefully cut up from the bottom of the cone and along the line.

5 Hold the two cones together and twist them around, snipping any awkward bits, until you get the closest fit—it really doesn't need to be perfect, so don't worry! Mark each piece with a pencil, so you know which sides meet up.

6 Brush a thick layer of tacky glue around the edge of each cone.

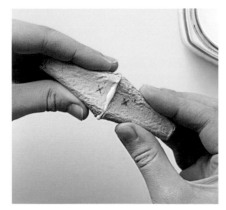

TIP

A second coat of glue should help fill any stubborn holes or, for a seamless finish, stick small pieces of newspaper over the join with watered-down glue (see page 8).

7 Push the cones together. Use the glue to fill any gaps. Leave to dry propped up in the egg-carton lid.

8 Paint the body blue-gray and white (as a guide, about a third of the body should be white), and paint the cereal-box cardboard blue-gray. This will be for the tail, fin, and flippers. If you want both sides of these painted, follow the instructions on page 9.

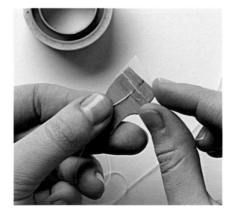

9 When the paint is dry, use the templates on page 123 to draw the tail, dorsal fin, and two flippers on the blue-gray cardboard. Cut these out.

10 Cut about 20 in. (50 cm) of thread for hanging the dolphin, then cut a small groove at the bottom of the dorsal fin to catch the end of the thread. Stick the thread down with some tape.

11 Hold the body steady and make a hole just behind the join on the top, with the small scissors, gently twisting and pressing to pierce through the thicker cardboard. Cut a slot through the join, long enough to fit the tab at the bottom of the dorsal fin. Wiggle the scissors in and out a little to make it easier to feed the tab through.

12 Mark and cut slots on either side of the body, just in front of the join for the flippers. Push them in.

13 Stick the tail tab on to the end of the body with tacky glue. Leave to dry, then bend back into place.

14 Use a black felt-tip pen to draw eyes and a big smile.

Silas the Shark

Not a peep from the deep when the shark's on his way. No fish wants to end up being dish of the day...

The shark's body is made the same way as the dolphin's (see page 84), and if you have any egg cartons with bigger cones, then this is a perfect time to use them!

1 Using scissors, roughly cut out two whole cones from the egg carton—this makes them easier to work with.

2 Using a pencil, make a mark on the cone just above the point where the join was in the egg carton.

3 Using a ruler or tape measure, check the measurement from the top of the cone, then use this to measure and mark all the sides and corners on both cones with the pencil. Join the marks by drawing a line.

You will need

Egg carton

Approx. 4 x 4 in. (10 x 10 cm) cereal-box cardboard

Small sheet of white paper

Mouth, tail, and fins templates (see page 125)

Small scissors (see page 8)

General-purpose scissors

Tacky glue (see page 8)

Blue and white paint

Paint brush

Approx. 20 in. (50 cm) white thread

Needle

Clear adhesive tape

Pencil

Ruler

Fine black felt-tip pen

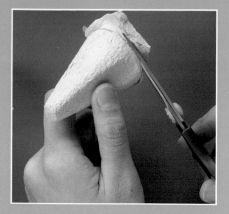

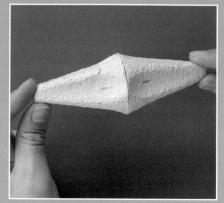

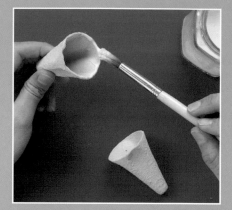

4 Carefully cut up from the bottom of the cone and along the line.

5 Hold the two cones together and twist them around, snipping any awkward bits, until you get the closest fit—it really doesn't need to be perfect, so don't worry! Mark each piece with a pencil, so you know which sides meet up.

6 Brush a thick layer of tacky glue around the edge of each cone.

7 Push the cones together. Use the glue to fill any gaps. Leave to dry propped up in the egg-carton lid.

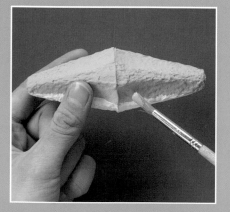

8 Paint the body blue and white (as a guide, about a third of the body should be white), and paint the cereal-box cardboard blue. This will be for the fins and tail. If you want both sides of these painted, follow the instructions on page 26.

9 When the paint is dry, use the templates on page 125 to draw the pectoral and dorsal fins and the tail. Cut these out.

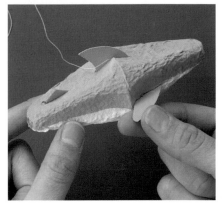

10 Cut about 20 in. (50 cm) of thread for hanging the shark, then cut a small groove at the bottom of the dorsal fin to catch the end of the thread. Stick the thread down with some tape.

11 Hold the body steady and make a hole just behind the join on the top, with the small scissors, gently twisting to pierce through the thicker cardboard. Cut a slot through the join, long enough to fit the tab at the bottom of the dorsal fin. Wiggle the scissors in and out. Make a cut in the same way near the tail for the second dorsal fin and slot that in.

12 Mark and cut slots on either side of the body, just in front of the join, for the pectoral fins, and push them in.

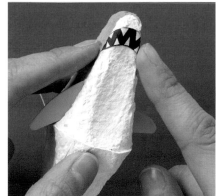

13 Stick the tail tab on to the end of the body with tacky glue. Leave to dry before bending back into place.

14 For the mouth, draw the mouth template on white paper. Using a fine black felt-tip pen, zigzag from top to bottom all the way along to draw the teeth. Go over this a few times to thicken it.

15 Cut out the mouth and glue on the underside of the shark's head. Draw small eyes and gills on the shark.

T.ish the Jellyfish

Swish, swish goes Trish, with her tentacles flowing.
She's really quite transparent and very easygoing.

You will need

Clear plastic egg carton

4 sheets of tissue paper in different colors

General-purpose scissors

Glue

Clear adhesive tape

Approx. 20 in. (50 cm) white thread

Needle

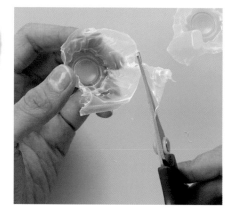

1 Cut a cup out of the egg carton, don't worry about the edge being neat—wavy is good for a jellyfish!

2 Thread the needle with enough thread to dangle your jellyfish, and push it up through the bottom of the egg cup, knotting or sticking the end in place inside the cup with some clear adhesive tape.

3 To make the tentacles, fold the sheets of tissue paper over a few times so that it is easy to cut across them.

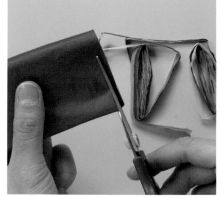

4 Cut off thin strips—three should be enough for one jellyfish—then separate the strips and lay them out together.

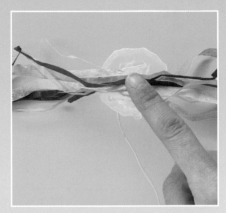

5 Put a good dab of glue inside the egg-cup piece, then gather the tissue strips in the middle and push them into the glue. Leave to dry.

6 When the glue is dry, scrunch up the tentacles and trim them to the length you want.

Otto the Octopus

The octopus gets so confused,
he's often in a fuddle.
Forgetting which is left and right,
with eight legs to unmuddle.

You will need

Egg carton

2 x 12 in. (30 cm) colored pipe cleaners

General-purpose scissors

All-purpose glue

Paint to match the color of the pipe cleaners, white paint

Paint brush

Cork (from a wine bottle or similar)

Fine black felt-tip pen

1 Cut out a cup from the egg carton, and use your thumbs to push up underneath to give it a more rounded shape on top.

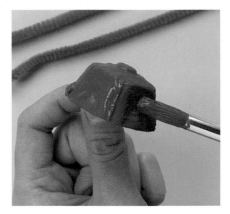

2 Paint this the same color as the pipe cleaners. Leave to dry.

3 To make the tentacles, cut the pipe cleaners in half, then bend each piece in the middle.

4 Spread a thick layer of glue inside the egg carton cup, then stick down the first tentacle piece, with the middle bend in the center. It can get rather sticky, so use the cork to push the pipe cleaners into the glue.

5 Lay another tentacle piece across the first one, dividing the egg carton cup into quarters, using the middle bend as a guide. Repeat with the other pieces until you have eight evenly spaced tentacles.

6 Bend over the sharp tips of the pipe cleaners to form the ends of the tentacles, and arrange as you like.

7 Dot on some white paint for eyes. When it is dry, use the fine black felt-tip pen to put a dot on each of the eyes and to draw the eyebrows and mouth. This octopus looks a little anxious!

Totally Turtles!

The turtles slowly swim along, they're always so sedate.
No point in going crazy when you're almost ninety-eight.

You will need

Egg carton

4 x 4 in. (10 x 10 cm) cereal-box cardboard or egg-carton lid

Head, flipper, and leg templates (see page 125)

Small scissors (see page 8)

Glue

Green and yellow paint

Paint brush

Ball of modeling clay

Black felt-tip pen

1 Cut out a cup from the egg carton and push up the bottom with your thumbs, smoothing out any corners so it looks more dome-shaped. This will be the turtle shell.

2 Paint the turtle shell and the piece of cereal-box cardboard or egg-carton lid green on both sides, then leave to dry.

3 Draw on a tortoise-shell pattern with the black felt-tip pen and then paint on some spots with the yellow paint.

4 Using the templates, draw a head, two back legs, and two curved front flippers on the green cardboard and then cut them out.

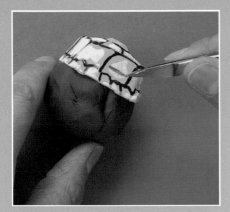

5 Mark a slot for the head about halfway up one side. Put a ball of modeling clay under the cup so there is something to push against. Use the small scissors to pierce through the card (keep closed, press down, and twist a little). Remove the ball of modeling clay. Cut a slot wide enough for the head tab—make it a little longer so the turtle can retreat into his shell if it all gets too much!

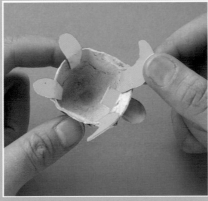

6 Add a face (you could do smiley one side, sad the other, if you like), and slot the head tab in.

7 Glue the legs and flippers underneath in the corners, and leave to dry upside-down, before bending into place.

Sneaky Stingrays

Stingrays use sand for camouflage, they're masters of disguise. You'd never ever spot them if it wasn't for those eyes!

You will need

Egg carton

4 x 2 in. (10 x 5 cm) cereal-box cardboard or egg-carton lid

Small scissors (see page 8)

General-purpose scissors

Glue

Paint in colors of your choice

Paint brush

Pencil

Ruler

Fine black felt-tip pen

The stingray is made from a section of the side of an egg carton where there's a curve from the cups for the flapping wings, and a raised middle bit for the body. All egg cartons have this basic shape—the edge of your egg carton or the middle join might be slightly different, but that's okay. Quite often the carton ends are the best source, because there's usually more card here, but this stingray is from the lid side, as there was a rounded edge, so it's always worth having a look.

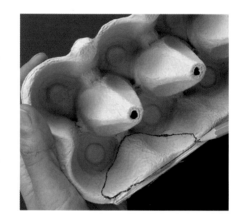

1 Once you've found your stingray shape, use a pencil to draw the outline and cut it out roughly with scissors. Then draw over the outline carefully and cut it out.

2 Paint this shape, plus the egg-carton lid or the cereal-box cardboard, whatever color you want. Leave to dry. This egg carton was already a lovely bright yellow, so it didn't need painting.

3 Once the cardboard is dry, use a ruler to draw an arrow, about 1½ times the length of the stingray body, that tapers to a point at the end. The arrow head goes under the back of the body with the side tips showing. If the shape of your egg carton means there's a gap at the back of the stingray, then make the arrow head bigger to fill it. Glue in place and leave to dry.

4 Using whichever color you like, paint spots on your stingray.

5 While that's drying, cut a thin strip of cardboard, and carefully round off both ends.

6 Cut about ½ in. (1 cm) from each end of the strip. Use a black felt-tip pen to add a dot next to the rounded edge of both pieces.

7 Mark slots big enough for the eyes on the raised middle part of the body, toward the front. Keeping the small scissors closed, press down and twist a little, until the point goes through the cardboard. Carefully snip the slots, and wiggle the scissors in and out to make it easier to push the eye tabs through.

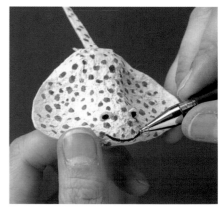

8 Use a fine black felt-tip pen to draw a wide smile.

Marvellous Manta Rays

They swim with their mouths open, it's really so easy to gather plankton on the go, no need to stop, you see!

You will need

Egg carton

4 x 2 in. (10 x 5 cm) cereal-box cardboard or egg-carton lid

Small scissors (see page 8)

General-purpose scissors

Glue

Blue-gray and white paint

Paint brush

Pencil

Ruler

Fine black felt-tip pen

Needle

Approx. 20 in. (50 cm) white thread

Clear adhesive tape

TIP
Like the stingray on page 96, the manta ray shape comes from the side of an egg carton, between cups. An end piece is best because there's more cardboard.

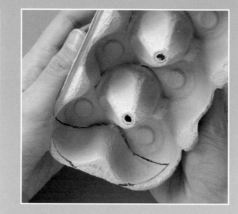

1 Using a pencil, sketch a manta ray shape on the area of egg carton you've selected. The wings should be pointier and longer than the stingray's, so you get more of an upward curve from the egg cup shape.

2 Use scissors to cut this shape out roughly. Then draw over the outline carefully, fine-tuning the shape if necessary to make sure the wings look even. Carefully cut around it.

3 Using the blue-gray color, paint just the top of the manta ray body, plus the egg-carton lid or the cereal-box cardboard. Leave to dry.

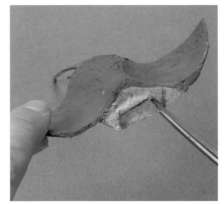

4 For the tail, use a ruler to draw an arrow on the cardboard. It should be about 1 ½ times the length of the body and taper to a point at the end. If necessary, adjust the size of the arrow head to fill any gap that might be left at the back of the body. Cut it out.

5 Glue in place with the bottom corners of the arrow head showing. Leave to dry.

6 On the small piece of cardboard at the front, between the wings, draw the manta ray's horns (used to direct plankton and water into its wide mouth), and snip out carefully. If there's not enough cardboard here, or the cutting is too fiddly, cut two little triangles from some spare cardboard and stick them underneath instead, or leave them out altogether.

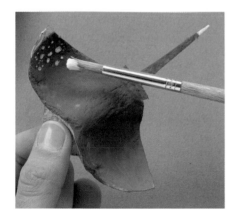

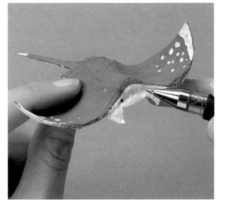

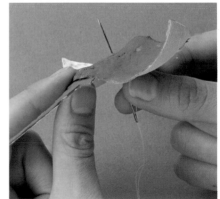

7 Paint the face and the underside of the body white and add some spots on top.

8 When dry, draw wide-apart eyes with a fine black felt-tip pen.

9 Thread the needle, tie a knot at the end of the thread, and push the needle up through the middle of the body. You may need to do this a few times to get the manta ray swimming the way you want! Use clear adhesive tape underneath if the knot isn't holding.

enclosures & scenery

Palm Tree

If you've ever made newspaper telescopes or a razzle-dazzle tree, then you'll know the rolling and pulling technique for making this palm tree.

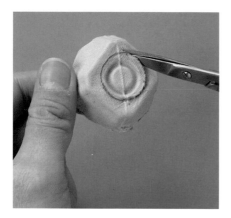

1 Cut out one cup from the egg carton and trim the edge so it sits flat and steady. Use small scissors to pierce the top and cut a round hole, about ¾ in. (2 cm) wide.

2 To make the tree trunk, roll the sheets of newspaper together. Don't roll too tight, but bear in mind it has to fit into the hole you've just made.

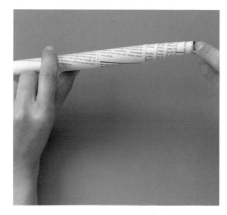

3 Hold the roll in one hand, and with the other, push up the inside of the roll from the bottom end, then pull up a middle piece from the top, gently twisting and loosening your grip on the roll a little as you do.

You will need

Egg carton

2 sheets of US Letter-size (A4-size) green paper

4 sheets of newspaper, each 8 × 12 in. (20 × 30 cm)

Small scissors (see page 8)

General-purpose scissors

Tacky glue (see page 8)

Brown paint

Paint brush

Small plate or bowl, approx. 8 in. (20 cm) in diameter

Pencil

Ruler

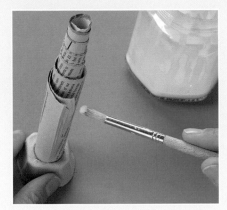

4 When the roll starts to narrow at the top and you've made some good ridges, cut off the bottom 4 in. (10 cm) or so, and push the top piece into the egg-cup base. Let the roll unfurl to fit before gluing the newspaper flaps down. Take the roll out, brush some glue around the edges of the hole, and stick the trunk back in place. Leave to dry.

5 When dry, paint the base and trunk brown. Don't use too much paint as seeing a few of the ridges adds to the palm-tree effect.

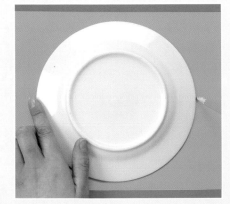

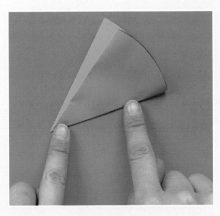

6 While the paint is drying, place the plate or bowl upside-down on a sheet of green paper and draw around it, then cut out the circle.

7 Fold the circle in half, then quarters, then eighths.

8 Fold one more time, just to make a crease down the middle, and open again. Measure ¾ in. (2 cm) up from the tip, draw a pencil line straight across, and make two marks on this line to divide it roughly into three.

9 Using the middle crease as a guide, draw a palm leaf in the center, from the top to the two marks at the bottom. Draw half a leaf on the folds either side, again from the top to the marks on the line.

10 Cut out carefully along the pencil lines and open up.

11 Cut just enough off the trunk top to make it flat. Brush some tacky glue in the center of the leaf circle and stick down. You can add another leaf circle for extra foliage, if you like.

Tree Times Three!

Trees with branches are a perfect hangout for the monkeys and birds. There are three different trees here, all straightforward, but if you're short of time, then Tree One is a good starting point.

Tree One

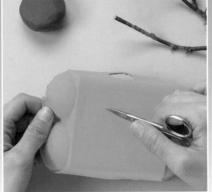

1 For a stand-alone tree scene, or a tree on a bank, paint an egg carton lid green, let dry, then make a small hole on top with the small scissors.

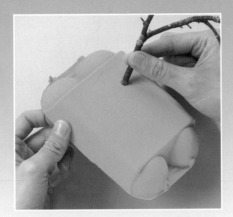

2 Put the ball of modeling clay under the hole in the lid and stick the twig down through the hole, into the clay.

You will need

Egg-carton lid

Small scissors (see page 8)

Small twig (preferably with an interesting shape)

Green paint

Paint brush

Small ball of modeling clay

3 If you like, add rocks or flowers from pages 110 and 111. To add leaves, use the techniques for Tree Two (see page 106) or Tree Three (see page 108).

Tree Two

1 Cut out one cup from the egg carton and trim the edge so it sits flat and steady. Paint this and the pieces of cardboard brown. Leave to dry, then pair up the pieces of cardboard and glue the shiny sides together. This will make your tree stronger. Leave to dry under a pile of books or something heavy.

You will need

Egg carton

2 pieces of cereal-box cardboard, each 10 x 11 in. (26 x 28 cm)

4 sheets of green tissue paper (in two different shades if possible)

Tree Two template (see page 125)

Small scissors (see page 8)

General-purpose scissors

Glue

Brown paint

Paint brush

Pencil

Ruler

2 Place the tree template on the card and draw around with a pencil. Cut it out. Repeat so you have two tree shapes. Younger children may need some help cutting through the double-thick cardboard.

3 Take one of the tree pieces and cut up the middle of the trunk until you're about ¾ in. (2 cm) from the top of the trunk. Snip away an extra sliver of card, to widen the slot a little.

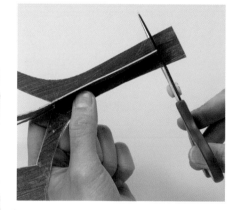

4 Push this piece over the other one, sliding it down as far as it will go. Trim the bottom of the tree, so both pieces are level. Pull apart again so you can add the leaves.

5 Put the sheets of tissue paper together, and loosely fold over a few times, then cut into thin strips.

6 Unravel the tissue-paper strips and tear them up a bit. Then brush plenty of glue on the tree tops, scrunch up a small handful of tissue-paper strips, and push them down on to the glue, making sure they cover the cardboard. Turn over and repeat on the other side.

7 Trim or glue in any very unruly strips, but leave some dangly, loose bits, too.

8 Draw a cross on top of the egg-cup base with a pencil. Use the small scissors to pierce through the card and cut along the lines. (If you'd like to add some grass around the bottom of the tree, see page 110.)

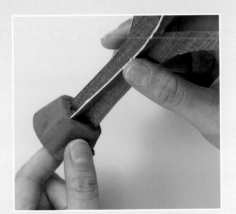

9 Slot the tree back together. The best way to get it through the cross is to push the egg cup flaps up from underneath with your fingers, while pushing in the trunk end with the other hand.

Tree Three

1 Make the trunk and the base of the tree by following steps 1–4 of the instructions for Tree Two (see page 106) but using the Tree Three template.

2 For the leaves, put the sheets of green paper together and fold over once. Use a spare piece of cereal-box cardboard to make a copy of the leaf template, and draw around this ten times down the folded side of the paper. Cut this strip out (keep the rest for future trees), before carefully snipping around the leaves with small scissors. You should end up with 40 leaves.

3 Dab a little glue on each leaf and decorate your tree. Leave to dry.

4 When dry, slot the tree back together and push into the egg-cup base, as described in Steps 8—9 of Tree Two. If you want to add some grass at the base of the tree, use the techniques on page 110.

You will need

Egg carton

2 pieces of cereal-box cardboard, each 10 x 11 in. (26 x 28 cm)

2 sheets of US Letter-size (A4-size) green paper in two different shades (or plain paper painted dark and light green)

Tree Three and leaves templates (see page 126)

Small scissors (see page 8)

General-purpose scissors

Glue

Brown paint

Paint brush

Pencil

Water

You will need

Cereal-box cardboard

General-purpose scissors

Glue stick

Blue paint

Paint brush

Plastic wrap (clingfilm)

1 For a pond or watering hole, use the scissors to cut out the shape you want from the cereal-box cardboard and paint it blue. Leave to dry.

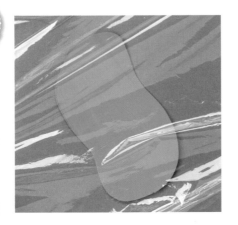

2 When it is dry, wrap a piece of plastic wrap around it. Cut away any excess plastic wrap underneath, so it sits flat.

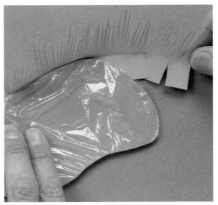

3 Use the glue stick to glue the plastic wrap securely under the cardboard. If you like, you can add rushes around the water, following steps 3–6 for making grass (page 110).

Grass

1 For a larger area of grass, to go inside an enclosure, measure how much paper you need to cover the base of the enclosure, and add about 1 in. (3 cm).

You will need
Green paper
General-purpose scissors
Glue
Ruler

2 Fold this extra bit over and snip long zigzags into it—vary the length and angle. Uneven is good! Glue into place.

3 For grass around rocks, trees, or water, decide what length you want the grass to be and add ½ in. (1 cm). Cut a strip of paper this size, and fold the ½ in. (1 cm) over. Snip a fringe of wavy grass into the longer bit. To position the grass around the edge of a rock or tree trunk, carefully make several snips along the ½ in. (1 cm) fold.

4 Wrap the grass around the rock or tree trunk and glue underneath. If you cut too far, or the strip rips, don't worry—just stick the pieces on separately.

Flowers

You will need
Colored tissue paper
General-purpose scissors
Glue

The small, colorful flowers are simply scrunched-up little squares of tissue paper. Fold a piece of tissue paper over a few times so you get several squares in one cut. Scrunch a few different colors together to jazz up your flowers. Glue into position wherever you want them.

Icebergs & Rocks

Painted egg-carton cups and cones make great icebergs and rocks.

Rock

You will need

Egg carton

Piece of white paper (for the iceberg)

General-purpose scissors

Tacky glue (see page 8)

White and black paint

Paint brush

Old plate for mixing paint

Pencil

1 Cut a cone and a cup from the egg carton. Using a pencil, mark a line straight up and across an egg cup piece, close to an edge. Cut this out. Fit the cup piece against a cone. Trim as needed and stick together with tacky glue. Leave to dry.

2 Put a small blob of black paint and a larger one of white either side of a plate, and mix in the middle. Splodge on the gray with dabs of black and white for a better rock effect.

Iceberg

1 Use the egg-carton lid for the base of a large iceberg. Cover any writing with a piece of white paper cut to size.

2 Cut five egg-cup pieces (or more, if you want to) from the egg carton. Make all the pieces different heights. Draw a line straight across the top of two of them, anywhere you like, then cut up and along the line. Carefully snip the sides off each one so they slope a little, and sit against the lid. Glue into place on the side of the egg-carton lid. Use tacky glue to fill any gaps.

3 To fit two egg-cup pieces together, sit a larger cup on top of a smaller one, and draw around the curve of the larger cup on top of the smaller one. Cut this curve out, and trim the sides at a slight slope, to fit against the larger cup. Glue in place with tacky glue. Leave to dry, then glue this and the last egg cup piece in to place wherever you want them on to the egg-carton lid. Add more egg-cup pieces to the side and top of the egg-carton lid if you want.

4 When you're happy with the shape of your iceberg, give it a few coats of white paint.

Basic Enclosure

If you don't want all your animals roaming free, you'll need to make them homes! Here and on pages 117 and 118 are ideas for zoo enclosures.

You will need

Cereal box

Colored or plain paper

Green tissue paper

General-purpose scissors

Glue

Glue stick (optional)

Brown, green, and blue paint, gray paint (optional), or color of your choice

Paint brush

Sandpaper

Pencil

Ruler

2 paperclips

Black felt-tip pen

1 Working around the edge so that the cardboard stays in one piece, cut the front off the cereal box. Don't cut off the flaps, as you'll need the side ones later for attaching the gate.

2 Cut the front piece in half, glue the shiny sides together, and weigh down under something heavy, like a pile of books, to dry.

3 Paint the enclosure base brown, green, or blue if it is to be a pool. The paint is splodged on here to make it look muddy—mix a little blue into the brown for some contrast.

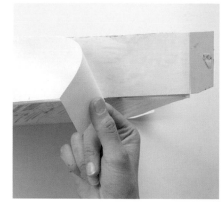 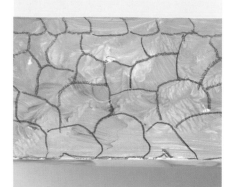 

4 If you want to paint the outside of the walls as well as the inside, either rub the shiny card with sandpaper so the surface is easier to paint (see page 9), or cover with plain or colored paper by cutting strips to fit and sticking to each side using a glue stick.

5 You can decorate the walls by painting them any color you like. Draw lines to make them look like fences, or you could try a stone-effect using gray paint, with stone shapes drawn in pen or pencil once the paint is dry.

6 For a hedge, tear up some green tissue-paper streamers (see page 106), brush a layer of glue on to the card, and press a small handful of streamers into the glue. Leave to dry and then trim with scissors.

 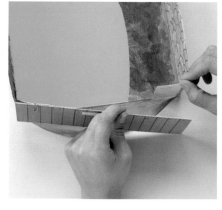 

7 If you want to add an area of grass to your enclosure, as here, follow steps 1–2 on page 110.

8 Cut a gate for your enclosure from cardboard you glued together in step 2—it will already be the right width. Trim the gate to make it the same height as the walls. Paint the gate, leave it to dry, then draw lines using a black felt-tip pen and ruler. Glue the gate to the front flaps. Use the paperclips to hold it in place while it dries.

9 Add some rocks, trees, and flowers (see pages 102–111), or anything else you want!

TIP

If you like, you can trim the sides of the cereal box. To cut the sides straight, measure the same distance from the base at various points around the sides and mark with a pencil. Draw a line connecting these marks and cut along the line.

You will need

Shoe box (or similar box)

Egg carton

Green and white paper

Green (optional), yellow, and orange tissue paper

Cereal-box cardboard

Baby birds template (see page 123)

Small scissors (see page 8)

General-purpose scissors

Glue

Blue, brown, black, yellow, and green paint (optional)

Paint brush

Pencil

Ruler

Needle

Clear adhesive tape

Aviary

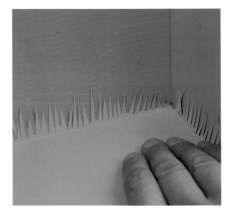

1 Stand the box upright and paint the inside blue, except for the base. Leave to dry then, using the green paper, cut out and glue some grass to the base (see steps 1–2 on page 110).

2 To add trees to the aviary, either paint a tree trunk and branches directly on to the sides of the box, or paint the piece of cereal-box cardboard brown, leave to dry, then cut out tree-trunk shapes and glue into position.

3 Cut out short branches from the painted cereal-box cardboard, and make slots for them through the trees, so your parrots (see page 70) have somewhere to perch. This should be done by an adult, as the shoe-box cardboard is likely to be tricky to pierce through. Cut small grooves on the parrots' sides, so they can slot on to a branch.

4 Using the green tissue paper, cut thin strips and glue some foliage (see pages 106–107) to the tree or paint this on, if you prefer.

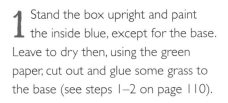

5 Design and decorate your bird house on a piece of white paper. Cut this out, as well as a roof and pole from some cereal-box cardboard. Glue all the pieces in place. Cut out an extra piece of card to make a handy bird table. Use the small scissors to make a slot below the bird house and insert the bird table.

6 To make a nest, cut a shallow egg cup out of the egg carton and paint it yellow. Leave to dry. Make yellow and orange streamers by folding pieces of tissue paper and cutting thin strips. Tear these up, cover the outside of the nest in glue, and press the streamers into it. Repeat on the inside.

7 Cut a slot along the bottom, using small scissors (keep closed, press down, and twist to pierce a hole). Make sure to snip part of the way up the sides too, so the nest can slot on to a branch.

8 Copy the baby birds template on to a small piece of spare cereal-box cardboard and cut it out. Paint it, bend the bottom tab back, and glue at the front of the nest. Add a few more streamers to cover the tab. Leave to dry, then slot onto a tree branch.

9 To attach your flying birds (see page 75), either stick the threads to the underside of the top of the aviary with clear adhesive tape, or thread a needle and push it up through the cardboard and fix in place on top with tape.

Aquarium

TIP
Use adhesive putty
(Blu-Tack®) to attach
your turtles and
stingrays to the back
of the aquarium, so you
can move them around.

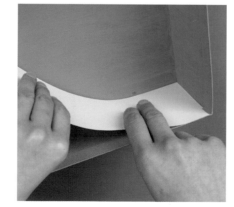

1 Use a shoe box or any other box you have. Lie on its side and paint all but the base blue. Paint that yellow, or cut some paper to fit, and glue in place using a glue stick.

2 Cut some strips of green tissue paper for seaweed. Use the glue stick to "draw" where you want the seaweed strands to go, then stick them down, at intervals, so they billow out and look floaty.

You will need

Shoe box (or similar box)

Cereal-box cardboard

Egg carton

Old greetings cards

Green tissue paper

Aluminum foil (optional)

Yellow paper (optional)

Small piece of foam sponge

Fish template (see page 123)

General-purpose scissors

Glue and glue stick

Blue, yellow, red, white, gray, and black paint

Paint brush

Pencil

Ruler

Clear adhesive tape

Needle

Approx. 20 in. (50 cm) white thread

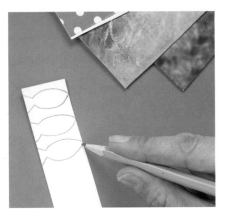

3 Use colorful old cards for the little fish. You can also use shiny cardboard to make your fish by gluing aluminum foil to cereal-box cardboard. Decide how long you want your fish to be, and cut a strip of card that width. With a pencil, draw fish shapes along the back of the card from the very bottom to the very top. Use the fish template (see page 123) as a guide.

4 Cut out the fish shapes and glue in place. Making shoals of different-sized fish is very effective.

5 For the coral, pull lumps out of the piece of foam sponge until you're happy with the shape.

6 Mix red and yellow paint and splodge this orangey color onto the sponge, dabbing on spots of yellow and red paint too. Finish with little touches of white paint.

7 To make a small rock cave, cut out an egg-carton cone and cut an opening in one side. Paint the outside of the cone gray and the inside black. Leave to dry, then glue on small fish.

8 If you've used a shoe box with a lid, you can use the lid to make a silver frame for the aquarium. Measure and draw a ¾ in. (2 cm) rim around the front of the lid. Cut out the middle section. Cut four strips of aluminum foil roughly to size, rub a glue stick over the cardboard frame, and wrap the pieces of foil around each side. Cover any corner gaps with small bits of foil.

9 To attach your swimming fish and jellyfish, either stick the threads to the underside of the top of the aquarium with clear adhesive tape, or thread a needle and push it up through the cardboard and fix in place on top with tape.

Zoo Entrance

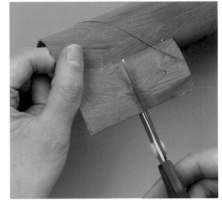

You will need

2 paper-towel (kitchen-roll) tubes

2¼ x 9 in. (6 x 23 cm) cereal-box cardboard

Old greetings cards

Pink and green tissue paper

"Zoo" letter templates (see page 126)

General-purpose scissors

Glue

Paint in the colors of your choice

Paint brush

Ruler

TIP

Why not add some bunting above the ticket office instead? Draw a line above the office, cut small colorful triangles from the greetings cards, and glue them to look like they're hanging from the line.

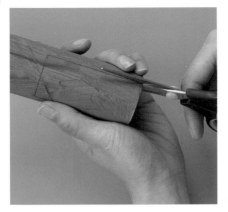

1 Paint the paper towel tubes any color you like. Leave to dry. To make the ticket office, on one of them, draw and cut a flap 3 x 1½ in (8 x 4 cm).

2 Bend the flap back and snip off the top 1½ in. (4 cm) to make a window.

3 To make a rambling rose, scrunch up little squares of tissue paper to make leaves and flowers (see page 110) and glue them around the ticket office. You can decorate the tubes any way you want —perhaps make a "Ticket Office" sign or make a few posters and glue them to the tubes. You can also draw lines to resemble panels on the ticket-office door and paint on a handle.

4 To make the "Zoo" banner, either paint the letters in the center of the piece of cereal-box cardboard banner, or use the templates to draw and cut the letters out of some colorful old greetings cards. Glue the letters to the center of the banner and leave to dry.

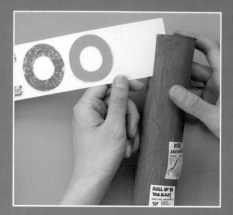

5 With the ticket office and posters (if you've made some) facing forward, measure and draw a 2¼ in. (6 cm) line from the top of each tube, opposite each other. Cut down each line to make slots and push the "Zoo" banner into position.

Templates

Some of the projects have templates to copy. There are a few different ways to use the templates: either copy freehand, trace them, or photocopy them. This last option is probably the easiest. Use a glue stick to glue a photocopied page on to a similar-sized piece of cereal-box cardboard and leave to dry under something heavy, like a pile of books. Roughly cut out the templates first, then neaten up each shape. Remember to label them, and keep them somewhere safe, so you can always make more. To speed things up, have a go at copying some of the small, simple-shaped templates freehand.

All templates are printed at 100%, so there is no need to enlarge them!

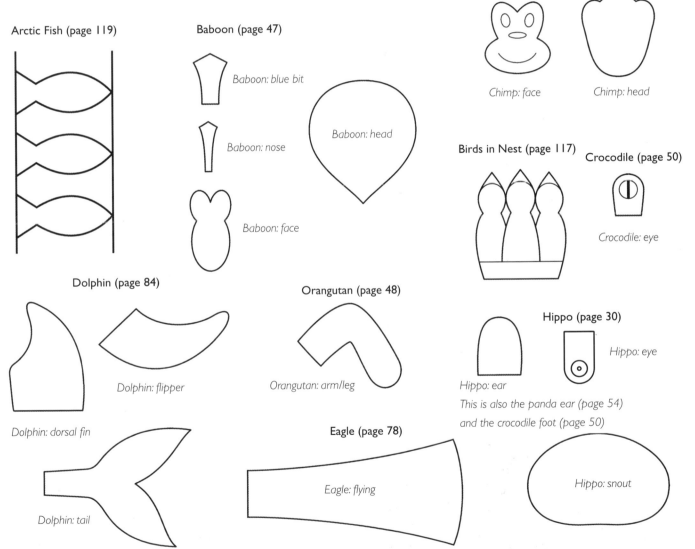

Arctic Fish (page 119)

Baboon (page 47)

Baboon: blue bit

Baboon: nose

Baboon: head

Baboon: face

Chimp (page 44)

Chimp: face

Chimp: head

Birds in Nest (page 117)

Crocodile (page 50)

Crocodile: eye

Dolphin (page 84)

Dolphin: flipper

Dolphin: dorsal fin

Dolphin: tail

Orangutan (page 48)

Orangutan: arm/leg

Eagle (page 78)

Eagle: flying

Hippo (page 30)

Hippo: eye

Hippo: ear

This is also the panda ear (page 54) and the crocodile foot (page 50)

Hippo: snout

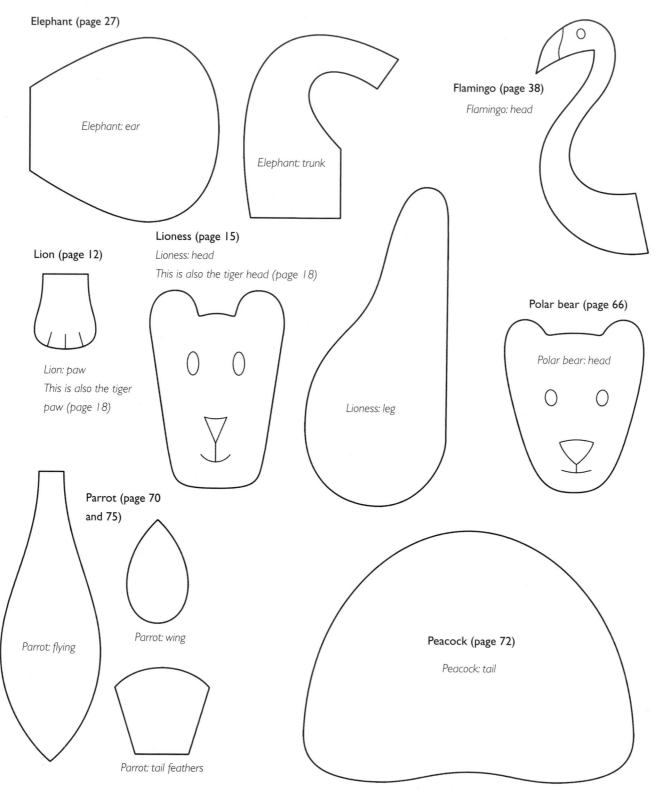

Elephant (page 27)

Elephant: ear

Elephant: trunk

Flamingo (page 38)

Flamingo: head

Lioness (page 15)

Lioness: head

This is also the tiger head (page 18)

Lion (page 12)

Lion: paw

This is also the tiger paw (page 18)

Lioness: leg

Polar bear (page 66)

Polar bear: head

Parrot (page 70 and 75)

Parrot: flying

Parrot: wing

Parrot: tail feathers

Peacock (page 72)

Peacock: tail

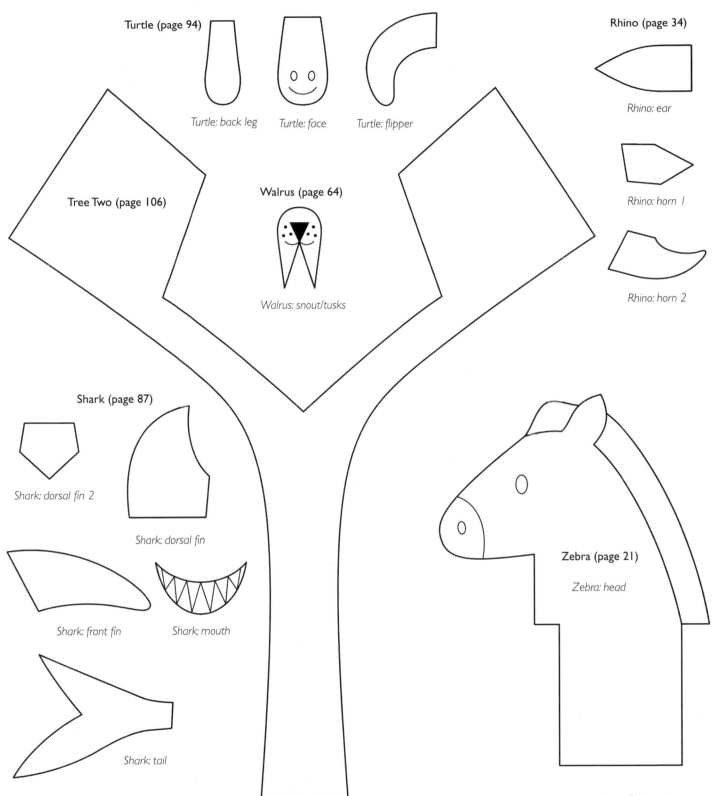

Turtle (page 94)

Turtle: back leg

Turtle: face

Turtle: flipper

Rhino (page 34)

Rhino: ear

Rhino: horn 1

Rhino: horn 2

Tree Two (page 106)

Walrus (page 64)

Walrus: snout/tusks

Shark (page 87)

Shark: dorsal fin 2

Shark: dorsal fin

Shark: front fin

Shark: mouth

Shark: tail

Zebra (page 21)

Zebra: head

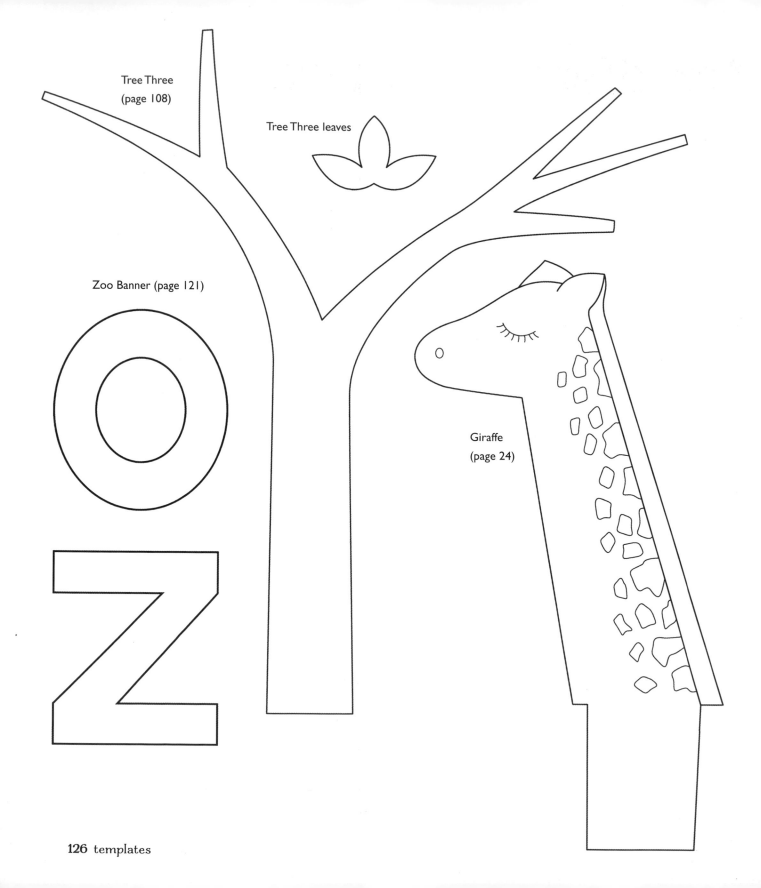

Tree Three
(page 108)

Tree Three leaves

Zoo Banner (page 121)

Giraffe
(page 24)

Suppliers

Index

bye!